The Lord Our Healer

An in-depth, comprehensive study on healing.

By

Dr. Steven E. Boate Ph.D

PRESS

Table of Contents

CHAPTER ONE

Renewing the Mind

What is the main reason or purpose for the Word of God? The main reason or purpose is to form beliefs. If we don't form beliefs from the Word of God, we will be governed by our senses, by our feelings, or by what others have to say. Now if the main purpose for the Word of God is to produce beliefs, what are the beliefs for? The main reason for beliefs is to govern our lives. When the Word of God is the final word for us, then it will cause us to believe, talk, and act like it is the final authority for us in all areas.

Before anyone can receive healing in his or her body, they need to get rid of all doubt as to whether it is the will of God to heal them. Doubt is the enemy of faith.

Romans 12:1-2
1 "I beseech you therefore, brethren, by the mercies of God, that you present your bodies a living sacrifice, holy, acceptable to God, which is your reasonable service. **2** And do not be conformed to this world, but be transformed by the renewing of your mind, that

you may prove what is that good and acceptable and perfect will of God."

Notice that it says for us to "renew our minds". Whether
we realize it or not, our minds are filled with all kinds of
beliefs from our parents, our schools, our friends, our
culture, and even our churches. Unfortunately, those beliefs
may be wrong. That is why this verse tells us to renew our
minds. We need to renew our minds to the Will or the Word
of God. Faith begins where the Will of God is known and
the Bible is God's Will for our lives. Unless we renew our
minds to the Bible instead of believing what others say, we
will miss out on the blessings of the healing power of God.
Renewing our mind is a process. What is a process?

Webster's Ninth New Collegiate Dictionary
defines process as "a continual forward
movement, a series of actions or measures. A
method of operation, a projecting part or
growth."

In other words, we are always renewing our mind to the
Word of God. It is an on-going process for the rest of our
lives. Ephesians 4:23 says: "and be renewed in the spirit of
your mind." I like how the Twentieth Century New
Testament puts it: "That the very spirit of your mind must be
constantly renewed." Notice the words "must" and
"constantly". It is a **must** to renew our mind to what the
Bible says about our healing, and we must **constantly** be
renewing our mind. If you need healing, that is the area to
which you must renew your mind. If we are not renewing
our minds in the area of healing, it will be to easy for our
enemy, the devil, to deceive us into thinking God's promises
of healing are not for everyone.

> According to W.E. Vines Expository Dictionary of New Testament Words, As a noun, he defines the renewed mind as: "An adjustment of the moral and spiritual vision and thinking to the mind of God which is designed to have a transforming effect upon the life."

For the Word of God to have a transforming effect in our spirits and minds, we must start thinking in line with what He says. To do this, we may have to adjust our thinking from the things we have been taught in school by our parents, by our friends, and even by some ministers.

"For who has known the mind of the LORD that he may instruct Him? But we have the mind of Christ." 1 Corinthians 2:16

The Amplified Bible puts it this way;

> "For who has known or understood the mind (the counsels and purposes) of the Lord so as to instruct Him and give Him knowledge? But we have the mind of Christ (the Messiah) and do hold the thoughts (feelings and purposes) of His heart."

Since we hold the thoughts of His heart, that would include healing for our mortal bodies. God is a healing God and He wants to heal you of every sickness, disease, or symptom that may be attacking your body. Matt 19:26 tells us: But Jesus looked at them and said to them, "With men this is impossible, but with God all things are possible." If God created the universe, the stars, the sun, the moon, the fish of the sea, the fowl of the air, (and He did); if He also parted the Red Sea for the children of Israel to pass through (and He did), don't you think He can heal your body?

Matthew 4:23
And "Jesus went about all Galilee, teaching
in their synagogues, preaching the gospel of
the kingdom, and healing all kinds of sickness and all kinds of disease among the
people."

Notice the word "all". All means "all". Let's look at
another scripture: Matthew 9:35, Then "Jesus went about all
the cities and villages, teaching in their synagogues, preaching the gospel of the kingdom, and healing every sickness
and every disease among the people."

Again, notice the words **healing every sickness and
every disease**. Every means every, and that includes you
and your sickness. Whatever you need to be set free from or
healed of, He is our deliverer and our healer. Jesus is the
same yesterday, today, and forever. He wants people totally
healed and set free by His unchanging power.

CHAPTER TWO

He Is the Same

Hebrews 13:8: "Jesus Christ the same yesterday, and today, and forever."(KJV) The Bible says Jesus is the same. He changes not. What He did in the past, in what is called the "Bible Days", when He walked with His disciples and healed people, He is still doing today, and He will continue healing people forever. Malachi 3:6a says "I am the Lord, I do not change."

These two verses tell us that God and Jesus do not change. What is the first word that comes to your mind when someone says they are the same all the time?

The word consistent comes to my mind. Webster's Ninth New Collegiate Dictionary says the word consistent means to show "steady conformity to character, profession, **belief**, or custom". As we study the Word we see that through the pages of the Bible the character of Jesus and His custom was going about and healing all who came to Him believing for their healing. His purpose and goals were always the same, that is to do the Father's will. John 5:30 "I can of Myself do nothing. As I hear, I judge; and My judgment is righteous, because I do not seek My own will but the will of the Father who sent Me."

Healing is a gift from God. A gift is something that someone gives to another free of charge, no strings attached. We do not have to earn it or work for it. It is a free gift. Gifts have to be received. When I receive a birthday gift or a Christmas gift, I did not have to work for it or earn it; I just had to receive it with thanksgiving.

James 1:17-18
"Every good gift and every perfect gift is from above, and comes down from the Father of lights, with whom there is no variation or shadow of turning."

Question, Is cancer good? Are tumors good? The answer is "no" to both questions. Therefore, all we need to do is receive His healing power into our lives as a free gift. Notice in Acts 10:38 "How God anointed Jesus of Nazareth with the Holy Spirit and with power, who went about doing good and healing all who were oppressed by the devil, for God was with Him."

Again, healing is a good thing and He went around healing all. All means all. I found that the Bible shows Jesus healing all who believed in Him for their healing. In other words, you get what you believe. If you believe God is a good God, and He wants you healed, you are on the right road. The next thing to know is that He is willing and able to heal all who ask, believe, and receive by faith. It is by faith that we receive our healing. He is our healer. He is the same and He never changes. Hebrew 13:8 "Jesus Christ the same yesterday and to day, and for ever."

Here is a quote from Barns. Jesus Christ the same yesterday ... As this stands in our common translation, it conveys an idea

which is not in the original. It would seem to
mean that Jesus Christ, the unchangeable
Savior, was the end or aim of the conduct of
those referred to, or that they lived to imitate
and glorify him. But this is by no means the
meaning in the original. There it stands as an
absolute proposition, that "Jesus Christ is the
same yesterday, today, and forever", that is,
that he is unchangeable. The evident design
of this independent proposition here is, to
encourage them to persevere by showing that
their Savior was always the same; that he
who had sustained his people in former
times, was the same still, and would be the
same forever. The argument here, therefore,
is that perseverance is founded on the
"immutability" of the Redeemer. If He were
fickle, vacillating, changing in his character
and plans; if today he aids his people, and
tomorrow will forsake them; if at one time he
loves the virtuous, and at another equally
loves the vicious; if he formed a plan yesterday which he has abandoned today; or if he
is ever to be a different being from what he is
now, there would be no encouragement to
effort. Who would know what to depend on?
Who would know what to expect tomorrow?
For who could have any certainty that he
could ever please a capricious or a vacillating being? Who could know how to shape
his conduct if the principles of the divine
administration were not always the same? At
the same time also, that this passage
furnishes the strongest argument for fidelity
and perseverance, it is an irrefragable proof

of the divinity of the Savior. It asserts immutability-sameness in the past, the present, and to all eternity but of whom can this be affirmed but God? It would not be possible to conceive of a declaration which would more strongly assert immutability than this."

No matter how you cut it up, slice it up, and dish it out, Jesus is not schizophrenic. He does not change. There is no sickness in heaven. As we study in the Old Testament, God did a great deal of healing. If God healed in the Old Testament and He healed in the New Testament times, why would He stop with us? It does not make sense for someone to say "healing has been done away with" because He is the same now and for always He "changes not".

CHAPTER THREE

Your Faith Has Made
You Whole

There is a story in the Bible about a woman who had an issue of blood for twelve years. She spent all that she had to get well, but she grew worse. She heard about Jesus and that He was going around healing people who came to Him believing that He would heal them. She knew from what she had heard that all she had to do was to touch the hem of His garment, and she would be healed. She pressed through the crowd to get to Him. She would not let anyone or anything get in the way of her receiving her healing. I call that determination!

Mark 5:25-34
25 "Now a certain woman had a flow of blood for twelve years, **26** and had suffered many things from many physicians. She had spent all that she had and was no better, but rather grew worse. **27** When she heard about Jesus, she came behind Him in the crowd and touched His garment; **28** for she said, "If

only I may touch His clothes, I shall be made well." **29** Immediately the fountain of her blood was dried up, and she felt in her body that she was healed of the affliction. **30** And Jesus, immediately knowing in Himself that power had gone out of Him, turned around in the crowd and said, "Who touched My clothes?" **31** But His disciples said to Him, "You see the multitude thronging You, and You say, "Who touched Me?" **32** And He looked around to see her who had done this thing. **33** But the woman, fearing and trembling, knowing what had happened to her, came and fell down before Him and told Him the whole truth. **34** And He said to her, "Daughter, your faith has made you well. Go in peace, and be healed of your affliction."

When Jesus spoke to her and said, "Your faith has made you whole", those same words are also for everyone who believes in His healing power. It is our faith. We can touch Jesus just like this woman did. How? By our faith in His written Word, the Bible. Verse twenty-six reads "And had suffered many things from many physicians. She had spent all that she had and was no better, but rather grew worse."

This woman knew a lot about suffering. She suffered from spending all her money; she suffered at the hands of doctors because they could not help her; and she suffered from people in society. Yet she never gave up hope. You may be in the same situation as she was. Don't give up because your faith in the healing power of God is present to heal you.

Now verse twenty-seven says "When she heard about Jesus, she came behind Him in the crowd and touched His garment." The Bible says in Romans 10:17 "Faith comes by hearing and hearing by the Word of God." She must have been hearing about Jesus for quite some time because she had the faith to receive. Faith comes from hearing and hearing the Word of God. So, when we keep the Word of God regarding healing in front of us and we keep hearing and hearing about healing, it builds faith in us to receive and act on what we believe. Case in point: When we were going through grade school and we did not know how to add or subtract, we kept going over it and over it and over it until it became a part of us. That is the same thing with the healing power of God.

Look at verse twenty eight, "For she said, If only I may touch His clothes, I shall be made well." She spoke what she believed. Then she said "I shall". The word "shall" is one of the strongest words in the English language. It is a knowing. I shall or I will be whole.

2 Corinthians 4:13: "And since we have the same spirit of faith, according to what is written, "I believed and therefore I spoke", we also believe and therefore speak." We need to speak the Word of God over our lives, more specifically, the Healing Word. We will do one or the other. We will speak life, faith and healing, or we will speak doubt and unbelief and keep the door closed for the Lord to heal us.

Proverbs 18:21 says "Death and life are in the power of the tongue, and those who love it will eat its fruit." Our words are containers and they will carry life, blessings and healing, or death, sickness, and disease. Matthew 12:37: "For by your words you will be justified, and by your words you will be condemned." I hear people saying things like, "God may not want me healed. He's trying to humble me and make me get closer to Him", How about this one, "This is my cross to bare, and I must carry my cross."

We need to understand that healing is a process. Just like when we scrape our elbow or knee, a scab will form and in time it will heal. It is the same with receiving the healing power of God. Healing takes time, whereas a miracle is instantaneous. There are a multitude of reasons why God wants us healed and the best place to find those reasons is in the Word of God. The Word of God has all the answers to your questions on healing.

CHAPTER FOUR

Reasons Why It Is God's Will To Heal

Reason 1) Because of God's original plan and creation.

> **Genesis 1:26,31**
> **26** Then God said, "Let Us make man in Our image, according to Our likeness; let them have dominion over the fish of the sea, over the birds of the air, and over the cattle, over all the earth and over every creeping thing that creeps on the earth."
> **31** Then God saw everything that He had made, and indeed it was very good. So the evening and the morning were the sixth day.

If it was very good, it means there was no sickness or disease because sickness and disease is not good. If we would have said to Adam and Eve, "I have a cold or Flu", they would have said "What's that"? If we would have said to them, "I have Cancer or a tumor", they would ask, "What's that"? There was no sickness, disease, death, decay, or corruption in God's original plan of creation. I know it is hard to imagine that because of all the sin and sickness in the world today, but this does not negate the fact that the original creation reveals the will of God. If sickness and disease pleased God and was part of His plan, He would have created it in the beginning. Well, if that is true, then where did sickness come from? I'm glad you asked.

Reason 2) The origin of sickness and disease is from the fall of man.

Sickness and disease is a manifestation of spiritual death working in our body and this is not the way God made it. Sickness and disease is the foul offspring of it's father Satan and it's mother Sin.

> (Guy P.Duffield/N.M. Van Cleave) Foundations of Pentecostal Theology writes "there is little room for disagreement that sickness is the result of the coming of sin into the world. Created as he was, In the image of God, if man had not sinned, he certainly would not have suffered pain, weakness, and disease in his body".

Paul makes it very clear that death is the result of sin. Romans 5:12 "Therefore, just as through one man sin entered the world, and death through sin, and thus death spread to all men, because all sinned."

> (Guy P. Duffield/N.M. Van Cleave) Foundations of Pentecostal Theology writes "Death is sickness matured. Death is the result of sin. Therefore sickness must also be the result of sin, since the greater (death) contains the lesser (sickness). This means

that if there had been no sin in the world there would have been no sickness."

We all know the story of Adam and Eve in the garden, when they ate of the forbidden fruit. That was the fall of man. The first sin man had ever committed was rebellion toward God.

Genesis 3:3 "but of the fruit of the tree which is in the midst of the garden, God has said, "You shall not eat it, nor shall you touch it, lest you die;"

> Verse 6 "So when the woman saw that the tree was good for food, that it was pleasant to the eyes, and a tree desirable to make one wise, she took of its fruit and ate. She also gave to her husband with her, and he ate."

Since that time, every person born into this world, is born with the same sin nature. That is why God sent Jesus into the world, to redeem us from the fall of Adam and Eve. Without Jesus in our lives we are helplessly hopeless.

John 3:16: "For God so loved the world that He gave His only begotten Son, that whoever believes in Him should not perish but have everlasting life."

People perish without Jesus; when they die they will end up in hell. The word "perish" also means that our bodies can and will be afflicted with sickness and disease. If a person has cancer, then that body is decaying with sickness and disease or it is perishing. We will discuss this issue in a later chapter. Sickness and disease is not from God. There is no sickness or disease in Heaven, and He does not afflict us with cancer, tumors, influenza, diabetes or anything else you can think of.

Matthew 7:11 "If you then, being evil, know how to give good gifts to your children, how much more will your Father who is in heaven give good things to those who ask Him!" I do not see God up in Heaven saying, I have Cancer; who would like this one"? NO! He is up in Heaven saying, "I have a gift called Healing; who would like this one"? Is your name on it? Will you take the gift of healing? Remember all sickness and disease is the result of the devil himself.

Reason 3) Sickness and disease is the work of the devil.

> **Job 2:7** "So Satan went out from the presence of the LORD, and struck Job with painful boils from the sole of his foot to the crown of his head." It says "Satan struck Job", not God. God does not put sickness upon us; He heals us.
>
> **Psalms 41:8** "An evil disease," they say, "clings to him. And now that he lies down, he will rise up no more." An evil disease comes from an evil devil.
>
> **Luke 13:16** "So ought not this woman, being a daughter of Abraham, whom Satan has bound, (think of it!) for eighteen years, be loosed from this bond on the Sabbath"? It says, "whom Satan has bound." If we are dealing with something in our body, we are held in bondage to it until we receive our healing. Fibromyalgia, arthritis, high blood pressure, insomnia, cancer and tumors are all from the devil and they put people in bondage. Acts 10:38 "How God anointed Jesus of Nazareth with the Holy Spirit and with power, who went about doing good and healing all who were oppressed by the devil, for God was with Him." We can clearly see

that all sickness and disease is the work of the devil. I like how one man put it: "Good God, bad devil". There is no good in the devil. There is no healing in him; in fact he is the author of all sickness. Notice it says, "Jesus was anointed with the Holy Spirit and with power, healing all who were oppressed by the devil." Sickness and disease is an oppression, but the good news is, that Jesus is still in the healing business, healing all who ask and believe in the healing power of the Lord. The Bible is a contract, or an agreement between God and man. It is better called "The Healing Covenant".

Reason 4) The Healing Covenant.

The word covenant means an agreement. An agreement has two sides to it. Some people think that if it is in the Old Testament, it doesn't apply to us today. That kind of thinking is simply not true. It is only true if in the Old Testament it has not been modified for the New Testament. An example from the Old Testament says in Exodus 21:23-25: "But if any harm follows, then you shall give life for life, eye for eye, tooth for tooth, hand for hand, foot for foot, burn for burn, wound for wound, stripe for stripe."

Matthew 5:38-44

38 "You have heard that it was said, "An eye for an eye and a tooth for a tooth." **39** But I tell you not to resist an evil person. But whoever slaps you on your right cheek, turn the other to him also. **40** If anyone wants to sue you and take away your tunic, let him have your cloak also. **41** And whoever compels you to go one mile, go with him two. **42** Give to him who asks you, and from him who wants to borrow from you do not turn away. **43** "You have heard that it was said, "You shall love your neighbor and hate your enemy." **44** But I say to you, love your enemies, bless those who curse you, do good to those who hate you, and pray for those who spitefully use you and persecute you."

So we can see that in this example the word has been modified from the Old to the New Testament. Now I will show you how the Old has not been modified.

Psalms 66:4

"All the earth shall worship You and sing praises to You; They shall sing praises to Your name."

Hebrews 13:15 "Therefore by Him let us continually offer the sacrifice of praise to God, that is, the fruit of our lips, giving thanks to His name."

So now we can see that praise and worship carried over to the New Testament was not modified or changed. We still praise and worship our God, and the Lord Jesus Christ.

So now back to the healing covenant.

Exodus 15:22-27

22 Then Moses led the people of Israel on from the Red Sea, and they moved out into the wilderness of Shur and were there three days without water. **23** Arriving at Marah, they couldn't drink the water because it was bitter (that is why the place was called Marah, meaning "bitter"). **24** Then the people turned against Moses. "Must we die of thirst?" they demanded. **25** Moses pleaded with the Lord to help them, and the Lord showed him a tree to throw into the water, and the water became sweet. It was there at Marah that the Lord laid before them the following conditions, to test their commitment to him, **26** "If you will listen to the voice of the Lord your God, and obey it, and do what is right, then I will not make you suffer the diseases I sent on the Egyptians, for I am the Lord who heals you". (TLB).

God does things on legal terms. The principles are the same even though the Old Testament was fulfilled by Jesus on the cross. Notice it says "If we listen to the voice of our God," which is His word, the Bible, then he says to obey His voice or the Bible. If someone was raising a child and they told that child "if you clean up your room I will take you out for ice cream", if the child does not obey, they don't get their treat. In the same way, if we don't obey the whole Bible, we don't have much to stand on.

Exodus 23:25 "So you shall serve the LORD your God, and He will bless your bread and your water. And I will take sickness away from the midst of you." The word "serve" has an implication of worship.

> Strong's Concordance 5647 `abad (aw-bad');
> a primitive root; to work (in any sense); by
> implication, to serve, till, (causatively)
> enslave, etc.: (KJV) - be, keep in bondage, be
> bondmen, bond-service, compel, do, dress,
> ear, execute, + husbandman, keep, labour
> (-ing man, bring to pass, (cause to, make to)

serve (-ingself,), (be, become) servant (-s),
do (use) service, till (-er), transgress
[from margin], (set a) work, be wrought,
worshipper

So it could read, "If you shall worship the Lord your God". How many people are truly worshipping the Lord our Healer? Many people are blaming Him instead of worshipping Him.

> Jesus said in **John 4:21-25**
> **21** Jesus said to her, "Woman, believe Me, the hour is coming when you will neither on this mountain, nor in Jerusalem, worship the Father. **22** You worship what you do not know; we know what we worship, for salvation is of the Jews. **23** But the hour is coming, and now is, when the true worshipers will worship the Father in spirit and truth; for the Father is seeking such to worship Him. **24** God is Spirit, and those who worship Him must worship in spirit and truth."

I truly believe if we will become true worshippers of Him, that healing will take place. Too many people are seeking the healing instead of seeking and worshipping the Healer, Jesus Christ, the Lord, our healer. Healing is in the covenant that God had with man. God the Father said, "If you will serve me or worship me, I will bless your bread and water and take sickness and disease away from you."

> **Deuteronomy 7:12-15**
> **12** "Then it shall come to pass, because you listen to these judgments, and keep and do them, that the LORD your God will keep with

you the covenant and the mercy which He swore to your fathers. **13** And He will love you and bless you and multiply you; He will also bless the fruit of your womb and the fruit of your land, your grain and your new wine and your oil, the increase of your cattle and the offspring of your flock, in the land of which He swore to your fathers to give you. **14** You shall be blessed above all peoples; there shall not be a male or female barren among you or among your livestock. **15** And the LORD will take away from you all sickness, and will afflict you with none of the terrible diseases of Egypt, which you have known, but will lay them on all those who hate you.

Notice the beginning of verse twelve, "Then it shall come to pass". The word "shall" is said to be one of the strongest words in the English language. Your healing shall or will come to pass because you listen, obey and keep the Word of God. Become a worshipper of God. Listen and obey the Word. Let me ask you these questions: Are you attending a church on a regular basis? Are you serving in your church? Are you paying your whole tithe to your church? Are you free from all unforgiveness? Are you free from strife and bitterness? Are you walking in love toward all people? These are all hindrances to receiving our total healing. If you leave one of these out, it is enough to stop the flow of healing into your body. I'm not saying it will, but it may. A lot of people think they need to keep the Ten Commandments, but the truth of the matter is that Jesus came and fulfilled them and gave us a new commandment to live by, and that is to walk in love. Romans 13:10 "Love does no harm to a neighbor; therefore love is the fulfillment of the law." If we are walking in love and forgiveness we are well pleasing to the father. 1 John 3:23 "And this is His commandment: that we should believe on the name of His Son Jesus Christ and love one another, as He gave us commandment." For the Lord to move on our behalf, we need to walk in love toward all. Some might say, "You don't know what they did to me". No, I don't, but look at what Jesus did for you, and He said to walk in love toward all. All is all, regardless of the situation. We do have a better covenant than the one started in the Old Testament.

> **Hebrews 8:6-7**
> But as it is, Christ has obtained a ministry which is as much more excellent than the old as the covenant he mediates is better, since it is enacted on better promises. For if that first covenant had been faultless, there would have been no occasion for a second. (RSV).

We have the same as the old, plus we have the Holy Spirit and the Name of Jesus Christ, the Anointed one and His anointing. We are better off than those under the Old Covenant. We are not just servants; we are sons and daughters of God and all the scriptures are true for us today. The new Covenant has a higher standard. If we walk in faith and love we are keeping God's covenant. The word covenant means an agreement between two people and in this case it is between God and you. Galatians 5:6 "For in Christ Jesus neither circumcision nor uncircumcision avails anything, but faith working through love." If you expect your faith to work for healing, then you must walk in love. Walking in love is a full time job. We need to be in the Word of God and praising Him on a continual basis, thanking Him for His love and forgiveness in our lives and asking Him to give us the strength and the ability from the Holy Spirit to love and forgive those who have hurt us and done us wrong.

Reason # 5) Healing belongs to us because sickness and disease is a curse of the law.

> **Galatians 3:13-14**
> Christ has redeemed us from the curse of the law, having become a curse for us (for it is written, "Cursed is everyone who hangs on a tree"), that the blessing of Abraham might come upon the Gentiles in Christ Jesus, that we might receive the promise of the Spirit through faith.

The word redeemed means to buy back. When I was a young boy, I would go and buy a Coke or Root-beer. In those days, when the bottle was empty you could take it back to the store and they would give you five cents. That is called "redeeming or buying back" and that is what Jesus did for us on the cross of Calvary through His death, burial, and resurrection. He redeemed us or bought us back from the hands of the devil. He bought us back from the curse of the law. There is a difference between the curse of the fall and the curse of the law. We have not been redeemed from the curse of the fall. The curse of the fall is pain in bearing children, working by the sweat of the brow, weeds and thistles. All these and more are the result of the curse of the fall. However we have been redeemed from the curse of the law.

> **1 Peter 1:18-19**
> **18** knowing that you were not redeemed with corruptible things, like silver or gold, from your aimless conduct received by tradition from your fathers, **19** but with the precious blood of Christ, as a lamb without blemish and without spot.

We were not redeemed by our own blood, or by our own strength but by the precious blood of Christ. He did for us what man could not do for himself.

Jesus shed His blood for you and me. It cost us nothing, but cost Him everything.

His blood is considered to be precious in 1 Peter 1:19. The word "precious" from Thayers Greek Lexicon is as follows:

> timios, timia, timion a. properly, held as of great price, i. e. precious: lithos, Rev 17:4 b. metaphorically, held in honor, esteemed, especially dear: Heb 13:4

We need to learn to honor, respect, and highly esteem His blood. There is power in His blood. Power to save, power to heal, power to deliver and set you free. Romans 1:16: "For I am not ashamed of the gospel, for it is the power of God for salvation to everyone who believes, to the Jew first and also to the Greek." (NASU) The Greek word for "power" is dunamis (doo'-nam-is) (where we get our English word dynamite); from NT:1410, force (literally or figuratively); especially, miraculous power (usually by implication, a miracle itself). that took place, the power, the force that took place when He shed His blood for us, saved us. The word "salvation" comes from a Greek word, "Soteria" (Strongs Concordance 4991), which comes from 4990, which is soter, from 4982, which is sozo and it means to save, deliver, or protect. (Lit or fig), heal, preserve, save, do well, be (make) whole.

So as you can see, healing, deliverance, and wholeness comes with our salvation, which came as a result of being redeemed from the curse of the law.

CHAPTER FIVE

Christ's Atonement

Isaiah 53:4-5
4 Surely He has borne our grief's and carried our sorrows; Yet we esteemed Him stricken, Smitten by God, and afflicted. **5** But He was wounded for our transgressions, He was bruised for our iniquities; The chastisement for our peace was upon Him, and by His stripes we are healed.

In Isaiah 53:4
"Surely He (Christ) has borne our grief's (kholee, sickness),and carried our sorrows (makob, pains)." Kholee (sickness) is from chalah, to be weak, sick, or afflicted. In Deuteronomy 7:15 we read, "the Lord will take away from thee all sickness (kholee)." This word is translated "sickness" in Deuteronomy 28:61, First Kings 17:17, Second Kings 1:2, Second Kings 8:8. Makob is translated "pain" in Job 33:19 "He

is chastened also with pain (makob)." In Jeremiah 51:18 we read, "take balm for her pain (makob)." Then Isaiah 53:4 should read "Surely He (Christ) has borne our sickness, and carried our pains."

The Verb in Isaiah 53:4 "born" (nasa) and "carried" (sabal). The Hebrew verb nasa means to bear in the sense of "suffering punishment for something." In Isaiah 53:12 We have the true meaning of nasa set forth: "And he (Christ) was numbered with the transgressors; and he bare (nasa) the sin of many." How did Christ bare our sins? Vicariously, as our Substitute. But this is the same verb used in Isaiah 53:4, "Surely He (Christ) has borne (nasa) our sickness." The same verb (nasa) is used of bearing our sins in Isaiah 53:12 as is used in Isaiah 53:4 of bearing our sickness.

1 Peter 2:24
Who Himself bore our sins in His own body on the tree, that we, having died to sins, might live for righteousness—by whose stripes (molopi, bruise) you were healed. Peter states that Christ bore our sins on the cross, and that by His stripes (literally bruise) you were healed. This agrees with Isaiah 53:5, which reads "But He was wounded on account of our sins, and was bruised because of our iniquities: the chastisement of our peace was upon him; and by his bruise (to molopi autou, by the bruise of Him) we are healed."

Notice it says in Isaiah 53:5 "by His stripes we are healed." And in 1 Peter 2:24 "by whose stripes you were healed." The prophet Isaiah was giving a prophecy to the cross, to what was going to take place, while Peter was looking back at the cross, at what had already taken place. In other words, if you were, then you are, if you are, then you were. It is forever settled in heaven that God sees us as healed because of the Atonement of Jesus Christ. Webster's Ninth New Collegiate Dictionary defines Atonement as "the reconciliation of God and man through the sacrificial death of Jesus Christ, the exemplifying of man's oneness with God."

We have been made one with the Father and the Son. John 17:23 says that "Jesus is in us and the Father is in Him, that we may be made perfect in one." The word "perfect" in the Greek is teleioo (tel-i-o'-o); from NT: 5046; to complete, i.e. (literally) accomplish, or (figuratively) consummate (in character).

In God's eyes, through the death, burial, and resurrection of Jesus Christ, we are complete in Him. No sin, sickness, or disease is in our life because we are complete in Him.

Numbers 21:5-9

5 And the people spoke against God and against Moses: "Why have you brought us up out of Egypt to die in the wilderness? For there is no food and no water, and our soul loathes this worthless bread." **6** So the LORD sent fiery serpents among the people, and they bit the people; and many of the people of Israel died. **7** Therefore the people came to Moses, and said, "We have sinned, for we have spoken against the LORD and against you; pray to the LORD that He take away the serpents from us." So Moses prayed for the people. **8** Then the LORD said to Moses, "Make a fiery serpent, and set it on a pole; and it shall be that everyone who is bitten, when he looks at it, shall live." **9** So Moses made a bronze serpent, and put it on a pole; and so it was, if a serpent had bitten anyone, when he looked at the bronze serpent, he lived.

Now jump on over to the New Testament in John 3:14,15

And just as Moses lifted up the serpent in the desert {on a pole}, so must {so it is necessary that} the Son of Man be lifted up {on the cross}, {Num. 21 9.} In order that everyone who believes in Him {who cleaves to Him, trusts Him, and relies on Him} may not perish, but have eternal life and {actually} live forever! (Amplified Bible).

This is clearly a type of Christ's sacrifice upon the Cross of Calvary. Just as the Israelites were healed as they looked upon the serpent on the pole, we too can be healed as we look to Jesus on the Cross. Sin and ignorance will bring sickness on us, as it did with the Israelites. They did repent and they got healed. As we repent, we also shall be healed.

Three things happened when they looked upon the serpent on the pole. They were forgiven; they were healed; and they were delivered. God took the snakes out.

I want to bring your attention back to Numbers 21:9 "So Moses made a bronze serpent, and put it on a pole; and so it was, if a serpent had bitten anyone, when he looked at the bronze serpent, he lived."

Now look at Hebrews 12:2: "Looking unto Jesus, the author and finisher of our faith."

The word, "looked" in Numbers 21:9 and the word, "looking" in Hebrews 12:2 have a connotation of a steadfast absorbing gaze. The reason why a lot of people do not get healed is, they do not keep their eyes in a steadfast absorbing gaze on 1 Peter 2:24. They get their eyes in a steadfast absorbing gaze on their sickness or disease. That will not work. We need to fix our eyes on Jesus and His Healing power until everything is better.

Jesus on the cross was representing the sin and death that He became for us. It would benefit us to take our eyes and minds off of our problem and fix them on what He did for us. We become what we behold, so keep your eyes on Jesus and the Word for your healing.

Abraham had to do the same thing.

Romans 4:19-21
19 And not being weak in faith, he did not consider his own body, already dead (since he was about a hundred years old), and the deadness of Sarah's womb. **20** He did not waver at the promise of God through unbelief, but was strengthened in faith, giving glory to God, **21** and being fully convinced that what He had promised He was also able to perform.

Notice he did not deny his body being old and dead. He just did not consider it. We have too many people saying, "there's nothing wrong with me"; I'm healed in Jesus name". We need to get our head out of the sand and be honest with ourselves. If the doctors say that I have a disease, then I will not deny it, but I will not consider it. I will consider what the Word says. We cannot receive our healing until we admit that we need healing. Abraham was considering the promises of God more than his body. He did not let unbelief and doubt creep in and chase the blessings away. He was strengthened in faith. How was he strengthened in faith? It tells us right there. He was giving glory to God for the promise that God gave him. He was fully convinced or persuaded that God was able to perform what he said He would do. We need to have that same conviction in our heart and mind.

CHAPTER SIX

The Passover Lamb

There are types and shadows in the Old Testament and it shows a clear picture of what was to come. God told Moses and Aaron to establish an ordinance, a pass-over to protect the Israelites and deliver them from certain plagues. Every man was to find a lamb without spot or blemish on the tenth day of the month. Then he was to watch over it for five days to make sure it is a perfect lamb.

On the fourteenth day of the month, he is to kill the lamb on his doorstep and catch the blood in a basin at the foot of his doorstep. This man is to take a hyssop bush, dip it in the blood and put some on the side of the door-posts and on the lintel of the house.

All this is to be done on the evening of the fourteenth day. The Hebrew day began at six o'clock in the evening. So that means they killed the lambs at three o'clock in the afternoon. That gave them three hours to do all this.

Exodus 12:1-14
1 Now the LORD spoke to Moses and Aaron in the land of Egypt, saying, **2** "This month

shall be your beginning of months; it shall be the first month of the year to you. **3** Speak to all the congregation of Israel, saying: 'On the tenth day of this month every man shall take for himself a lamb, according to the house of his father, a lamb for a household. **4** And if the household is too small for the lamb, let him and his neighbor next to his house take it according to the number of the persons; according to each man's need you shall make your count for the lamb. **5** Your lamb shall be without blemish, a male of the first year. You may take it from the sheep or from the goats. **6** Now you shall keep it until the fourteenth day of the same month. Then the whole assembly of the congregation of Israel shall kill it at twilight. **7** And they shall take some of the blood and put it on the two door-posts and on the lintel of the houses where they eat it. **8** Then they shall eat the flesh on that night; roasted in fire, with unleavened bread and with bitter herbs they shall eat it. **9** Do not eat it raw, nor boiled at all with water, but roasted in fire, its head with its legs and its entrails. **10** You shall let none of it remain until morning, and what remains of it until morning you shall burn with fire. **11** And thus you shall eat it: with a belt on your waist, your sandals on your feet, and your staff in your hand. So you shall eat it in haste. It is the LORD's Passover. **12** For I will pass through the land of Egypt on that night, and will strike all the firstborn in the land of Egypt, both man and beast; and against all the gods of Egypt I will execute

judgment: I am the LORD. **13** Now the
blood shall be a sign for you on the houses
where you are. And when I see the blood, I
will pass over you; and the plague shall not
be on you to destroy you when I strike the
land of Egypt. **14** So this day shall be to you
a memorial; and you shall keep it as a feast
to the LORD throughout your generations.
You shall keep it as a feast by an everlasting
ordinance.

This is not your normal everyday go the park barbecue.
There are thousands of men killing these lambs and putting
the blood on the door-posts and then roasting them. Imagine
what your city would smell like if this was being done
today. We would have to get a burn permit.
Verse five says the lamb is to be without blemish, a
male. Jesus was a male without spot or blemish.

1 Peter 1:18-20
18 knowing that you were not redeemed with
corruptible things, like silver or gold, from
your aimless conduct received by tradition
from your fathers, **19** but with the precious
blood of Christ, as of a lamb without blemish
and without spot. **20** He indeed was foreor-
dained before the foundation of the world,
but was manifest in these last times for you.

The last sentence says Jesus was manifested in these last
times for you. Aren't you glad that He came for you? It also
says that His Blood is precious, without spot or blemish.
Just as God was instructing Aaron and Moses to speak to
the congregation of Israel, saying "get a male lamb without
spot or blemish to sacrifice it for the use of the blood", Jesus

was sent by God to be our sacrifice and to shed His blood for us.

1 Corinthians 5:7 "Therefore purge out the old leaven, that you may be a new lump, since you truly are unleavened. For indeed Christ, our Passover, was sacrificed for us".

Before Passover, all the leaven had to be removed from their homes. The leaven was to represent their life of bondage in Egypt. So they had to remove all the leaven from their homes before they could commune with God.

Leaven is symbolic of sin. (biblically speaking) We need to make sure we are clean before we can enter the most Holy Place and commune with our Heavenly Father. God cannot be in the same room with sin. The way we become clean is by using 1 John 1:9, "If we confess our sins He is faithful and just to forgive us of all our sins, and to cleanse us from all unrighteousness" making us clean and pure in His presence.

There are two things God instructed them to do. Exodus 12:7 says "to take of the blood and apply it to the two doorposts and the lintel of the house where they eat of it."

In verses 8-11, He is talking about eating the flesh and how to eat of it. In verse eleven God says "it is the Lord's Passover".

Verse thirteen goes on to say, "Now the blood shall be a sign for you on the houses where you are. And when I see the blood, I will pass over you" (or protect you). Verse fourteen says this is to be a memorial, as a feast to the Lord for all generations; it is an everlasting ordinance.

Exodus 12:21-24
21 Then Moses called for all the elders of Israel and said to them, "Pick out and take lambs for yourselves according to your families, and kill the Passover lamb. **22** And you shall take a bunch of hyssop, dip it in the

blood that is in the basin, and strike the lintel and the two door-posts with the blood that is in the basin. And none of you shall go out of the door of his house until morning. **23** For the LORD will pass through to strike the Egyptians; and when He sees the blood on the lintel and on the two door-posts, the LORD will pass over the door and not allow the destroyer to come into your houses to strike you. **24** And you shall observe this thing as an ordinance for you and your sons forever.

When the Lord was crucified they pierced His side and blood and water came out. They also gave Him sour wine on a branch of hyssop.

John 19:29,34 29 "Now a vessel full of sour wine was sitting there; and they filled a sponge with sour wine, put it on hyssop, and put it to His mouth".

34 "But one of the soldiers pierced His side with a spear, and immediately blood and water came out".

We can clearly see the connection between the Old Testament and the New Testament for the Passover Lamb. This is a direct connection between a lamb without spot or blemish being used in the Old Testament and what Jesus our Lamb without spot or blemish did for us on the cross of Calvary.

Praise God we don't have to look for a lamb without spot or blemish as they did in the Old Testament for the forgiveness of our sins, for the healing of our bodies, or for protection against Satan and his army. Jesus paid the price once and for all. We can all take in a big breath and say "Praise God".

The Passover Lamb is connected to the Lord's Supper in:

1 Corinthians 11:23-31
23 For I received from the Lord that which I also delivered to you: that the Lord Jesus on the same night in which He was betrayed took bread; **24** and when He had given thanks, He broke it and said, "Take, eat; this is My body which is broken for you; do this in remembrance of Me." **25** In the same manner He also took the cup after supper, saying, "This cup is the new covenant in My blood. This do, as often as you drink it, in remembrance of Me." **26** For as often as you eat this bread and drink this cup, you proclaim the Lord's death till He comes. **27** Therefore whoever eats this bread or drinks this cup of the Lord in an unworthy manner will be guilty of the body and blood of the Lord. **28** But let a man examine himself, and so let him eat of the bread and drink of the cup. **29** For he who eats and drinks in an unworthy manner eats and drinks judgment to himself, not discerning the Lord's body. **30** For this reason many are weak and sick among you, and many sleep. 31 For if we would judge ourselves, we would not be judged.

CHAPTER SEVEN

Rightly Discerning the Lord's Body

Just as God told Aaron and Moses what to do with the Passover Lamb, (He instructed them to take the blood and apply it to the door post and overhead of their homes, and to eat of the flesh), so the Lord has told us to do two things in the Lord's Supper in 1 Corinthians 11:23-30. Drink of the cup and eat of the bread.

The reason a lot of people don't receive their healing is because they are not rightly discerning the Lord's body. We need to discern and understand why we take communion at Church, home, or wherever we take it so that we can receive His provisions of forgiveness and healing.

If you asked most people why they drink of the cup, they would tell you it is for the forgiveness of sins, and rightly true. If you asked them why they eat of the bread, you would get a lot of different answers.

1 Corinthians 11:23-31
23 For I received from the Lord that which I also delivered to you: that the Lord Jesus on

the same night in which He was betrayed took bread; **24** and when He had given thanks, He broke it and said, "Take, eat; this is My body which is broken for you; do this in remembrance of Me." **25** In the same manner He also took the cup after supper, saying, "This cup is the new covenant in My blood. This do, as often as you drink it, in remembrance of Me." **26** For as often as you eat this bread and drink this cup, you proclaim the Lord's death till He comes. **27** Therefore whoever eats this bread or drinks this cup of the Lord in an unworthy manner will be guilty of the body and blood of the Lord. **28** But let a man examine himself, and so let him eat of the bread and drink of the cup. **29** For he who eats and drinks in an unworthy manner eats and drinks judgment to himself, not discerning the Lord's body. **30** For this reason many are weak and sick among you, and many sleep. **31** For if we would judge ourselves, we would not be judged.

Verse twenty-four, Jesus is talking about eating of the bread, which is symbolic of His body and His flesh. He said to "do this in remembrance of Him", what He did on the cross. Verse twenty-five talks about the cup. This is symbolic of His blood; for the New Covenant which He made for us. Again He said, "do this in remembrance of Him", what He did for us. Verse twenty-six says, "as often as we do this we proclaim His death till He comes." And He is coming back again.

Why did He separate the two? The blood is for the remission and forgiveness of sins and eternal life. The Body is for the health and healing of the physical body.

In verse twenty-seven, it mentions of eating of the bread and drinking of the cup in an unworthy manner and being guilty of the body and blood of the Lord. In and of ourselves we are unworthy but His blood has made us worthy. Sin should not keep us from taking of communion but should make us run to the communion table because He shed His blood to cleanse us from our sin. Verse twenty-eight says, to examine ourselves. Most people misunderstand this as meaning to examine ourselves if we have sin in us. But the fact of the matter is that the Corinthians were making a feast out of the Lord's Supper and Paul was rebuking them and telling them that the Lord's Supper was not to be a feast or dinner for them, but a remembrance proclaiming the Lord's death till He comes back.

First Corinthians 11:29 "For he who eats and drinks in an unworthy manner eats and drinks judgment to himself, not discerning the Lord's body."

> **1 Corinthians 11:29**
> "For anyone who eats and drinks without discriminating and recognizing with due appreciation that {it is Christ's} body, eats and drinks a sentence (a verdict of judgment) upon himself". KJV-Amplified Parallel Bible.

(NASB) puts it this way, "If he does not judge the body rightly.

We can clearly see that we need to rightly discern the Lord's body. 1 Peter 2:24 "Who Himself bore our sins in His own body on the tree, that we, having died to sins, might live for righteousness, by whose stripes you were healed."

It says by His stripes we were healed. That is what I call rightly discerning and judging the main reason for taking the bread or wafer during the communion service at Church. By His stripes I am healed; I will claim it from the rooftops, even if my body does not feel like it. The Word is true and I will rightly discern the Lord's broken body for my healing.

"It is this careless participation which is the reason for the many feeble and sickly Christians in your Church." The New Testament in Modern English. 1 Corinthians 11:30 "For this reason many are weak and sick among you, and many sleep." In the Bible, sleep is a common metaphor for death. (Nelson's Illustrated Bible Dictionary), According to this verse, those who do not rightly discern the Lord's body can and will be weak, sick, and even die an early death.

If the body of Christ, the Church, would just realize the power and effect of the stripes that Jesus took on His back for our healing, deliverance, and restoration, those who would believe in that power without doubting and wavering, we would see a lot more people being healed and set free by His Anointing and power.

The Lord yearns to heal us and set us free, but we need to rightly discern and judge Him faithful to watch over His word to perform it in our lives.

CHAPTER EIGHT

Healing is the Children's Bread

This fits well with the teaching on Communion. The receiving of the physical bread serves as a point of contact for us receiving healing. It is a type of spiritual bread.

Matthew 15:21-28
21 Then Jesus went out from there and departed to the region of Tyre and Sidon. **22** And behold, a woman of Canaan came from that region and cried out to Him, saying, "Have mercy on me, O Lord, Son of David! My daughter is severely demon-possessed." **23** But He answered her not a word. And His disciples came and urged Him, saying, "Send her away, for she cries out after us." **24** But He answered and said, "I was not sent except to the lost sheep of the house of Israel." **25** Then she came and worshiped Him, saying, "Lord, help me!" **26** But He answered and

said, "It is not good to take the children's
bread and throw it to the little dogs." **27** and
she said, "Yes, Lord, yet even the little dogs
eat the crumbs, which fall from their masters
table." **28** Then Jesus answered and said to
her, "O woman, great is your faith! Let it be
to you as you desire." And her daughter was
healed from that very hour.

Jesus referred to healing and deliverance as the children's bread. What is He talking about? Healing and deliverance is the children's bread. Are you a child of the King?
Are you a child of God? If you are born again the answer to
both of these questions is "yes". That means healing and
deliverance is your bread.

Some people would have you think that Jesus is denying
her request and being totally rude and unloving. But that's
not the case here. Verse twenty-two says, "And behold, a
woman of Canaan came from that region and cried out to
Him, saying, "Have mercy on me, O Lord, Son of David!
My daughter is severely demon-possessed". This woman
was not a Jewish proselyte. She had not converted to being a
Jew. She didn't even serve Jehovah God. She was not a
Christian. She was unsaved in our standards. She was a
Canaanite woman. They were ungodly people. When she
came to the Lord, she did not come to receive the Lord, but
to ask Him to heal her daughter.

She came to Him asking for mercy. Even those who
claim they don't believe in Him still come to Him asking for
mercy and grace in their darkest hour. She was asking on
behalf of her daughter and not for herself. Jesus was moved
with compassion when He saw sick people.

This is a clear picture of how people are still the same-
give me, give me, give me. People run to God to get their
healing, then they forget about Him and go play with all

their toys. We need to fall in love with Him. Someone once said "we need to seek the healer and not the healing." Jesus said in Matt 6:33 "But seek ye first the kingdom of God, and his righteousness; and all these things shall be added unto you". (KJV)

If we go to Him for Him, love Him for Him, worship Him for Him, we will get our healing. Be more concerned about what He wants from you than what you want from Him and you will not lose out on your healing

Matthew 15:24
Jesus said, "I was not sent except for the lost sheep of Israel." "Israel." NT:2474 (is-rah-ale'); of Hebrew origin [OT:3478]; Israel (i.e. Jisrael), the adopted name of Jacob, including his descendants (literally or figuratively): (KJV) – Israel.

Jesus was saying that He came for the lost sheep or Children of Israel and this woman was a Canaanite. Notice in verse twenty-five "then she came and worshiped Him, saying, Lord, help me!" She truly knew that Jesus was the Lord; she humbled herself before the Lord. There is a direct connection between humility and healing. We need to stay humble before our Lord.

Being humble is simply letting the Lord know that without Him you are helpless and you need Him as your Lord and Savior. We need to fall in love with the one who created us in the likeness of His own image.

Also it is amazing when there are tragedies and hardships in peoples lives, how they seem to turn to the Lord for help. There have been people who come to our church for a season and then leave and go somewhere else where the teaching is not the same beliefs as ours, when they are in need of God for deliverance or healing for themselves or someone else, they will call us for prayer, just like this woman. She knew who to turn to and she worshipped Him.

If you ever want the Lord to do a miracle or heal your body, it would be a good idea to start out worshipping Him. Worship moves the hand of God.

> **Acts 16:25-26**
> **25** And at midnight Paul and Silas prayed, and sang praises unto God: and the prisoners heard them. **26** And suddenly there was a great earthquake, so that the foundations of the prison were shaken: and immediately all the doors were opened, and every one's bands were loosed. (KJV)

I found that when things are not going well in my ministry or my life, I start worshipping the Lord more and He always comes through. God is not moved by our tears, crying, and complaining, but He is moved by faith when we start worshipping Him. I don't mean worshipping Him in church on Sunday mornings, or for a few moments at home, but for a few hours at a time. Turn your phones off. Put a "do not disturb" sign on your front door and have yourself a good time worshipping the Father. You will see the answer to your prayers much quicker.

Matthew 15:26 "But He answered and said, "It is not good to take the children's bread and throw it to the little dogs."

The term "dogs" means puppies or little house pets. They lived like dogs eating off the street, whatever they could find. Jesus was saying, it was not good to take what belonged to the chosen ones and give to a Canaanite woman who lived like the dogs.

Matthew 15:27 And she said, "Yes, Lord, yet even the little dogs eat the crumbs which fall from their masters' table."

She was admitting the fact that she was a dog and lived

like a dog, but notice how she stayed after it and she says, "All I need are a few crumbs". Being humble with a heart of worship will bring the answer your way. That's called persistence-not giving up. We have to set our mind and heart like flint.

Most people give up after a day or two. They say, "this faith and healing stuff doesn't work". No, we have to stay at it with everything we have. Most people will work two and sometimes three jobs for a year or more to buy the toys they want or go on vacation. When it comes to the things of God, they give up too easily.

Hebrew 6:12 "That you do not become sluggish, but imitate those who through faith and patience inherit the promises."

Faith and patience go hand in hand. You can not have one without the other. We need more patience when it comes to standing for our healing. We need to stay in faith and not give up because your healing is right around the corner and you will receive your healing.

Matthew 15:28 "Then Jesus answered and said to her, "O woman, great is your faith! Let it be to you as you desire." And her daughter was healed from that very hour."

James 4:8 "Draw near to God and He will draw near to you. Cleanse your hands, you sinners; and purify your hearts, you double-minded."

We need more than ever, to draw near to Him. He loves you more than you will ever know. As we draw near to Him, He will draw near to us. You do not draw near to God just to get your healing, but because you love Him and you want to worship Him.

We are to stay persistent on standing on the promises of God's Word for our healing.

Ephesians 6:10-11 "Finally, my brethren, be strong in the Lord and in the power of His might. Put on the whole armor of God, that you may be able to stand against the wiles of the devil."

We are to put on the whole armor of God. Why? So that we may stand against the wiles, schemes, devices, or attacks of the enemy, the devil. And notice it says to "be strong in the Lord". We only have so much strength of our own and then we run out. We are to stay strong in the Lord and what He has done for us.

Ephesians 6:14 "Stand therefore, having girded your waist with truth, having put on the breastplate of righteousness".

What is truth? The truth is that we are healed. No matter what our bodies say to us or what the doctors say. You may have a ton of doctors' reports that say there is no hope. The doctors are giving you the truth from the natural and what they have been taught. The real truth though, is the Word of God. So having done all that you can do for yourself, stand on the Word of God.

CHAPTER NINE

Paul's Thorn in the Flesh

2 Corinthians 12:7-10
7 And lest I should be exalted above measure by the abundance of the revelations, a thorn in the flesh was given to me, a messenger of Satan to buffet me, lest I be exalted above measure. **8** Concerning this thing I pleaded with the Lord three times that it might depart from me. **9** And He said to me, "My grace is sufficient for you, for My strength is made perfect in weakness." Therefore most gladly I will rather boast in my infirmities, that the power of Christ may rest upon me. **10** Therefore I take pleasure in infirmities, in reproaches, in needs, in persecutions, in distresses, for Christ's sake. For when I am weak, then I am strong.

"One of the most prevalent objections raised today against the ministry of healing is Paul's thorn in the flesh. One traditional idea has led to another. "The widespread teaching that God is the author of disease, and that some of the most devout of His children He has desired shall remain sick, and glorify Him by exhibiting fortitude and patience, no doubt has led to the idea that Paul had a sickness that God refused to heal". (Christ the Healer F.F Bosworth).

Numbers 33:55-56

55 But if you do not drive out the inhabitants of the land from before you, then it shall be that those whom you let remain shall be irritants in your eyes and thorns in your sides, and they shall harass you in the land where you dwell. **56** Moreover it shall be that I will do to you as I thought to do to them.

Here the Bible tells us that the irritants in the eye and the thorns in the side of the Israelites were the inhabitants of Canaan and not an eye disease or sickness.

Joshua 23:13

Know for certain that the LORD your God will no longer drive out these nations from before you. But they shall be snares and traps to you, and scourges on your sides and thorns in your eyes, until you perish from this good land which the LORD your God has given you.

Have you ever heard the statement, "they're such a pain in the neck"?

That does not mean that every time you see that person that you get a pain in your neck. It is simply an idiom.

God is saying the same thing. They will be a problem to you and will get on your case or back, so to speak; they will harass you.

I used to have a neighbor living next door to me. He kept the outside of his home looking like a junkyard. It upset me to the point of planting bushes on our property line to hide his home. I would tell my wife that our neighbors home is an eyesore. It makes our home look dumpy. Did that mean I had sores in my eyes? Of course not. It is a figure of speech.

All three of the cases prove that the thorns are personalities. In the case of Paul, he said that the thorn was a messenger of Satan. The word messenger is the Greek word "Angelos" for angel. It was the angel of Satan, or as others have put it, the angel of the devil, or Satan's angel that was buffeting him.

Paul himself said it was a messenger of Satan. What does a messenger do? They deliver a message or a package of some kind. Well, this one brought all kinds of buffeting. So what is buffeting? NT: 2852 kolaphizo (kol-af-id'-zo); from a derivative of the base of NT: 2849; to rap with the fist: (KJV) – buffet.

The devil was trying to stop Paul from doing what God had called him to do. Everywhere Paul went, demonic spirits followed him, trying to stop what God wanted him to do. That is also true for us today. So many people will say something like this. Do you think God is trying to get your attention, or you may be out of God's will? No! No! No! If you are doing the will of God, the devil will do anything in his power to stop you. He will bring sickness and disease or whatever he can put upon you to try to buffet you.

Paul was beaten repeatedly. That was his thorn in the flesh. Not an eye disease or any other disease. As you study the life of Paul, you will find out that he was shipwrecked, imprisoned, and beaten for the work of the Lord.

Everything that Paul went through was because he

believed in what he was proclaiming and would not give into the pressures of the doubters and religious people of his time.

2 Corinthians 6:4-10
4 But in all things we commend ourselves as ministers of God: in much patience, in tribulations, in needs, in distresses, **5** in stripes, in imprisonments, in tumults, in labors, in sleeplessness, in fastings; **6** by purity, by knowledge, by longsuffering, by kindness, by the Holy Spirit, by sincere love, **7** by the word of truth, by the power of God, by the armor of righteousness on the right hand and on the left, **8** by honor and dishonor, by evil report and good report; as deceivers, and yet true; **9** as unknown, and yet well known; as dying, and behold we live; as chastened, and yet not killed; **10** as sorrowful, yet always rejoicing; as poor, yet making many rich; as having nothing, and yet possessing all things.

Matthew 10:14-23
14 And whoever will not receive you nor hear your words, when you depart from that house or city, shake off the dust from your feet. **15** Assuredly, I say to you, it will be more tolerable for the land of Sodom and Gomorrah in the day of judgment than for that city!
16 "Behold, I send you out as sheep in the midst of wolves. Therefore be wise as serpents and harmless as doves. **17** But beware of men, for they will deliver you up to councils and scourge you in their synagogues. **18** You will be brought before

governors and kings for My sake, as a testimony to them and to the Gentiles. **19** But when they deliver you up, do not worry about how or what you should speak. For it will be given to you in that hour what you should speak; **20** for it is not you who speak, but the Spirit of your Father who speaks in you. **21** Now brother will deliver up brother to death, and a father his child; and children will rise up against parents and cause them to be put to death. **22** And you will be hated by all for My name's sake. But he who endures to the end will be saved. **23** When they persecute you in this city, flee to another. For assuredly, I say to you, you will not have gone through the cities of Israel before the Son of Man comes.

Jesus said, if we would follow Him and teach His word that there would be hard times or persecution, but nowhere did He say we would be afflicted with any kind of eye disease or any other disease or sickness.

When Paul was asking God to take away the messenger of Satan, God told Paul that His grace was sufficient. Just as God's grace was sufficient for Paul, His grace is sufficient for us. We need to remember that God is full of grace and mercy. When we call upon Him, He is faithful. When we are weak then He is strong through us.

Romans 8:37: Yet in all these things we are more than conquerors through Him who loved us.

We are more than conquerors because the conqueror lives in us, and "Greater is He that is in us, than he that is in the world".

So you might be thinking, What about Job? Did not God afflict Job?" Is that what you heard? Let us take a look at the book of Job. I will bring you up to date in a paraphrased way. Here is a man who fears and worships and honors God like you would not believe. He has seven sons and three daughters and a whole lot of possessions. He was a very wealthy man.

> **Job 1:7,8**
> **7** And the LORD said to Satan, "From where do you come?" So Satan answered the LORD and said, "From going to and fro on the earth, and from walking back and forth on it." **8** Then the LORD said to Satan, "Have you considered My servant Job, that there is none like him on the earth, a blameless and upright man, one who fears God and shuns evil?"

In verse seven Satan says he has been going back and forth on the earth. He was trying to find someone he could destroy. And in verse eight the Lord says have you considered my servant Job. Satan says of course I have but you have a hedge about him and I can't get to him. Verse ten, but if you take down that hedge he will curse you to your face. Satan tried to get God to pull the hedge down.

Job 1:12, So the LORD said to Satan, "Behold, all that he has is in your power; only do not lay a hand on his person." So Satan went out from the presence of the LORD.

Satan didn't even know that the hedge was down, Job pulled the hedge down himself by being in fear. You see God permitted Satan to afflict Job just like He permitted Adam to sin and fall. But it was Adam's choice to fall into sin. Permission is not commission. We are free moral beings with a free will and choice of our own.

He told Adam don't do it. If you do, you will die. And Adam, like so many people today, did what the Lord said not to do. And then we pay the price for it dearly. You see obedience is better than sacrifice. We need to obey the Lord in all areas of our life. By not obeying we are opening the door for the devil to do what he wants to do in our lives. So Job let down the hedge and opened the door to the devil and the devil had a hay day with him. Satan started afflicting Job.

Job 1:20-22
20 Then Job arose and tore his robe and shaved his head, and he fell to the ground and worshiped. **21** And he said: "Naked I came from my mother's womb, And naked shall I return there. The LORD gave, and the LORD has taken away; Blessed be the name of the LORD." **22** In all this Job did not sin nor charge God with wrong.

People make this statement all the time, "the Lord gives and the Lord takes away". This is not an accurate statement. God did not do that to Job; Satan did it. But Job thought that God did it, so he blamed God-like a lot of people do today.

Job didn't rashly accuse God, but he didn't know anybody else to blame so he said, "the Lord gives and the Lord takes away". God allowed it because Job, like us, had the free choice of will; he was a free moral agent.

As long as Job walked in faith, worshipped God, trusted and believed in God, the hedge stayed up. But when Job got into fear and doubt and unbelief, the hedge came down. So he let the hedge down through his doubting.

1 Peter 5:8 "Be sober, be vigilant; because your adversary the devil walks about like a roaring lion, seeking whom he may devour". The devil is moving throughout the earth to see whom he can attack, and get away with it. We are to resist him when the attacks come our way.

Job 3:25 "For the thing I greatly feared has come upon

me, And what I dreaded has happened to me". Job said the thing he feared came upon him. First of all, he was in fear. Fear is of the devil, therefore, it is sin. He got what he was afraid of and also as he spoke. Proverbs 18:21 "Death and life are in the power of the tongue, And those who love it will eat its fruit". Second, he spoke his disaster into existence.

There are forty-two chapters in the book of Job. By reading this book, you would think that this was talking about his whole life. Hebrew scholars tell us that the whole book of Job took place in a nine to twelve month time span. As you study the book of Job you will find out that it did not take him all that time to get healed. Once he repented and got right with God and prayed for his friends, God restored to him all that was taken away and gave back double. Job 42:10 "And the LORD restored Job's losses when he prayed for his friends". Indeed the LORD gave Job twice as much as he had before.

So next time you are going through some tough times and somebody says your life is that of Job's, just say, "Praise God". What God did for Job by giving him twice as much, how much more will our Heavenly Father do for us when we get right with Him. Repent and forgive others and watch the healing power of God work in your life.

CHAPTER TEN

Different Ways to Receive Healing

One thing I have learned about God, He is God and He can bring forth a healing in any form He wishes. People tend to put Him in a box and they say things like God can only heal this way or that way.

I will share eight different ways to receive your healing.

(1) Pray for yourself

Mark 11:24 "Therefore I say to you, whatever things you ask **when you pray**, believe that you receive them, and you will have them". This verse says that we are to believe that we have the answer to our prayer when we pray. So if I need healing and I pray for myself, I am to believe that I have received my healing when I prayed. James 5:13 "Is anyone among you suffering? **Let him pray**. Is anyone cheerful? Let him sing psalms".

Again, I can pray for myself. This is the highest way or the best way to receive your healing, but it is not the only way.

(2) Have someone pray for you.

James 5:16 "Confess your trespasses to one another, and **pray for one another, that you may be healed.** The **effective,** fervent prayer of a righteous man avails much".

Notice it says effective. The only way our prayers can be effective is if we pray in line with the Word of God. "If it be thy will" is not in line with the Word of God.

Matthew 18:19 "Again I say to you that if two of you agree on earth concerning anything that they ask, it will be done for them by My Father in heaven". You do not have to be an ordained minister; you don't need anyone that is an ordained minister; all you need is someone who will agree with you on what God's Word says about healing. It says "where two agree on earth". If just two people are in agreement about anything it will be done. Would that include healing? Yes. Human thinking says, if I can get a thousand people praying I know God will hear and move. But the Word says if two of you agree. You may get a thousand people praying, but are they all in agreement with you and the word. Some may believe "if it is God's will", and yet others will think "maybe God does not want to heal", yet others will say "I hope so". That's not faith and they are not in full agreement with you or the Word of God.

(3) Ask in Jesus name.

John 14:13-14 "And whatever you ask in My name, that I will do, that the Father may be glorified in the Son. If you ask anything in My name, I will do it". We need to ask the Father in Jesus name. Too many people are asking God or the Holy Spirit, but Jesus said to ask the Father in His name. The word, "ask", in this verse has a connotation of demanding. We are not to demand anything from God or Jesus, but we are to demand or command the devil in Jesus name. We have a right to demand our bodies to be healed in Jesus name.

Mark 16:17-18
17 And these signs will follow those who believe: In My name they will cast out demons; they will speak with new tongues; **18** they will take up serpents; and if they drink anything deadly, it will by no means hurt them; they will lay hands on the sick, and they will recover.

Notice it says in "Jesus name". It is not in the name of your pastor, best friend, or anyone else for that matter. It is all in the name of Jesus.

(4) Ask the father in Jesus name.

John 16:23-24
23 And in that day you will ask Me nothing. Most assuredly, I say to you, whatever you ask the Father in My name He will give you. **24** Until now you have asked nothing in My name. Ask, and you will receive, that your joy may be full.

When Jesus said in that day, what day was He talking about? First of all, He was talking about the day when He was no longer here on the earth, but in heaven with His Father. It also refers to us now. Praying to the Father in Jesus name is for us today. We don't need anyone to do our praying for us. We can go straight to the throne room of grace ourselves. Hebrew 4:16 "Let us therefore come boldly to the throne of grace, that we may obtain mercy and find grace to help in time of need". Healing is a need, isn't it? That means He will give you grace and mercy in time of need if we go to the throne room.

We need to learn that there is power in the name of

Jesus. We all can admit that Jesus was full of power. His name and faith in His name has the same power as if He were here on earth. Kenneth E. Hagin said that "the name of Jesus" is the key that unlocks the door to the impossible and supernatural". Phil 2:10 "That at the name of Jesus every knee should bow, of those in heaven, and of those on earth, and of those under the earth". Sickness and disease **must,** I said **must** bow at the name of Jesus. There is no greater power than the name and blood of Jesus.

(5) Calling on the elders of the church and anointing with oil.

> **James 5:14-16**
> **14** Is anyone among you sick? Let him call for the elders of the church, and let them pray over him, anointing him with oil in the name of the Lord. **15** And the prayer of faith will save the sick, and the Lord will raise him up. And if he has committed sins, he will be forgiven. **16** Confess your trespasses to one another, and pray for one another, that you may be healed. The effective, fervent prayer of a righteous man avails much.

Is any sick? God has no favorites. He will heal any and all. Notice it says for the sick person to call on the elders of the church. Too many people leave a church if the pastor does not call them to see how they're doing. The word says we the sick are to call for prayer. It's not that the pastor and elders don't care; they're busy and they may not even know your sick. Also, it is a step of faith when we ask for help and prayer. The elders would come and pray the prayer of faith over the sick person and if need be, anoint with oil.

Oil is symbolic of the Holy Spirit. It does not say that

the oil will heal, but the prayer of faith. Too many people have their faith in the oil instead of the power of prayer and faith in the Word of God and the name of Jesus.

While I am on the topic-Oil is oil. It really does not matter what kind of oil you use, be it motor oil, cooking oil, or oil from the Holy Lands. Like I said, it is symbolic.

(6) By the laying on of hands

Mark 16:15-18
15 And He said to them, "Go into all the world and preach the gospel to every crea-ture. **16** He who believes and is baptized will be saved; but he who does not believe will be condemned. **17** And these signs will follow those who believe: In My name they will cast out demons; they will speak with new tongues; **18** they will take up serpents; and if they drink anything deadly, it will by no means hurt them; they will lay hands on the sick, and they will recover".

There is nothing said about using oil here. Jesus said, "in His name we are to lay hands on the sick and they will recover."

All believers can lay hands on the sick. We are not the healer. He is the Healer working through us. We are the tools or instruments through whom God has chosen to work. This is where most people are in their faith with God. They believe if so-and-so lays hands on them they will be healed. It's not the best way, but it is a way of receiving healing in your body.

Quite a few people have asked Brother Hagin this question. What if I'm not healed? His response is "if you were healed, you wouldn't have to believe it. If it were manifested, you would know it then, wouldn't you? But if you will take the step of believing that it is done, then you will receive it, because the principle of the prayer of faith is found in Mark 11:24 Therefore I say to you, whatever things you ask when you pray, believe that you receive them, and you will have them."

"Believe that you have received your healing and what will happen? You will have it! You see, the having comes after the believing." (Seven Things You Should Know About Divine Healing. Kenneth E. Hagin)

The laying on of hands can be explained this way. It is a form of contact and transmission. Jesus said to lay hands on the sick. The reason means the same thing, because we as believers are anointed by God and the anointing flows through our hands to the one who needs healing. Jesus operated in this way most of the time and as a rule I like to follow His example.

> Matthew 8:14-15 "Now when Jesus had come into Peter's house, He saw his wife's mother lying sick with a fever. So He touched her hand, and the fever left her. And she arose and served them".

> Mark 6:5 "Now He could do no mighty work there, except that He laid His hands on a few sick people and healed them".

> Mark 8:23 "So He took the blind man by the hand and led him out of the town. And when He had spit on his eyes and put His hands on him, He asked him if he saw anything".

> Luke 4:40 "When the sun was setting, all those who had any that were sick with various

diseases brought them to Him; and He laid His hands on every one of them and healed them".

Luke 5:13 "Then He put out His hand and touched him, saying, "I am willing; be cleansed." Immediately the leprosy left him".

Luke 13:13 "And He laid His hands on her, and immediately she was made straight, and glorified God".

Today when believers lay hands on the sick, they are being used by God as if it were Jesus himself laying hands on people. This is a basic Bible Doctrine.

Hebrew 6:1-2
1 Therefore, leaving the discussion of the elementary principles of Christ, let us go on to perfection, not laying again the foundation of repentance from dead works and of faith toward God, **2** of the doctrine of baptisms, **of laying on of hands**, of resurrection of the dead, and of eternal judgment.

(7) Special Miracles through handkerchiefs and aprons.

Acts 19:11-12
11 Now God worked unusual miracles by the hands of Paul, **12** so that even handkerchiefs or aprons were brought from his body to the sick, and the diseases left them and the evil spirits went out of them.

These were unusual miracles because Paul had no

scriptural reason for doing this outside of being led by the Holy Spirit. Today we call them prayer cloths, and many churches use them today. We need to understand that just as oil has no real virtue in it, it is the same with the cloth. It is the prayer of faith that is prayed over the cloth that gets the job done. It is like laying hands on someone, It is a point of contact to receive our healing.

Most of the time prayer cloths are used for home bound people or those who live too far to get to a meeting, or maybe someone in a hospital.

(8) Receiving by the Gifts of Healings.

1 Corinthians 12:8-11

8 for to one is given the word of wisdom through the Spirit, to another the word of knowledge through the same Spirit, **9** to another faith by the same Spirit, to another gifts of healings by the same Spirit, **10** to another the working of miracles, to another prophecy, to another discerning of spirits, to another different kinds of tongues, to another the interpretation of tongues. **11** But one and the same Spirit works all these things, distributing to each one individually as He wills.

One of the gifts God has placed in the body of Christ is the gifts of healings.

This is a supernatural manifestation of healing power going from one person to another. Notice in verse nine, the word "gifts" and "healings" are plural. There are many different ways that the Holy Spirit will bring a manifestation forth to bless someone with healing. Notice in verse ten it mentions the working of miracles. Miracles are different than healing. A miracle is an instantaneous healing, also changing the course of nature. A miracle would be replacing a body part such as a gall bladder once it had to be removed or being born without that body part. In verse eleven it states, as the Spirit wills. We can not wake up in the morning and say, "I think I will operate in the gift of miracles today". No, it is as the Spirit wills.

All these methods are good and scriptural, but the best way is knowing the Word of God and standing on 1 Peter 2:24, Isaiah 53:4-5, Matthew 8:17. Healing belongs to you. The Word says, "by His stripes you were healed".

CHAPTER ELEVEN

Why Some Do Not Get Healed

Did you notice I said, "why some do not get healed"? I did not say that God doesn't heal some. I said, some do not get healed.

Let me explain! If you saw someone walking down the street that you knew was not a Christian, would you say it was God's fault or their fault? We all know that it is each person's responsibility to be saved. It is the same with healing.

If there is a problem, it is on the receiving end and not on the giving side.

I have shared that it is the will of God for all to be healed. I will be sharing more about that, but right now I will show many reasons why some don't receive their healing. This is not a full list of reasons, but it will give you a good base to stand on.

(1) Lack of knowledge

Hosea 4:6 "My people are destroyed for lack of knowledge. Because you have rejected knowledge, I also will reject you from being priest for Me; Because you have forgotten the law of your God, I also will forget your children".

A lack of knowledge will keep us from receiving any answer to our prayers. It may be healing, or may be finances, or anything else for that you may need. Your faith will only rise to the level of your knowledge of the Word of God. The hand of faith reaches out and says "I have it now". If it's not faith, then it is wishing and hoping. That is why it is important to be in the Word and study the Word for your healing.

(2) Unbelief and doubt.

Matthew 13:58 "Now He did not do many mighty works there because of their unbelief".

Everywhere Jesus went, He healed people who came to Him asking and believing for healing. Then He comes to His own hometown; it says He could not do many mighty works because of their unbelief. The reason for this is they knew Him as a child. He grew up playing with the kids like we do. They knew he was the son of Joseph. They did not believe who He said He was-The Son of the Living God. Think about that. Jesus, full of the Holy Spirit and the anointing, could not heal people because of their unbelief and doubt.

Doubt and unbelief are the enemies of faith. And like I said, "faith is the hand that reaches out and receives healing." Once we have the knowledge that it is the will of God for all to be healed, then we have the choice to accept it or doubt it, but it is our choice. Sad to say too many preachers are putting doubt and unbelief in the hearts and minds of Christians.

Deuteronomy 30:19 "I call heaven and earth as witnesses today against you, that I have set before you life and death, blessing and cursing; therefore choose life, that both you and your descendants may live;"

I call being healed a blessing and not a curse. Therefore we are to choose healing. Some call sickness and disease a blessing. That is one blessing I choose not to have. Again, it is our choice.

One of the things God has given us is the free choice of will. We can basically do what we want in the confines of the law. We can choose not to get up in the morning and go to work, or we can choose to go to work. We can choose to live with someone outside of marriage and lose out on the blessings of God, or we can get married and receive the blessings of God in our marriage.

Preachers are always telling people that they need to be in church as much as possible, like every time the door is open. It is those people who complain about all the problems they are going through-marriage, physical, emotional, financial and occupational-yet they don't understand the devil is keeping them out of church to rob them of receiving what they need. The anointing of the Spirit and the Word of God will destroy the works of the devil. They always have some kind of excuse, but in all honesty, it's their choice. They are the ones who are always in trouble. That, my friend, is another reason why people don't get healed.

There are lots of examples in the Word of God that show a person's choice for receiving healing in their body. One in mind is the man they lowered through the roof of a home.

Mark 2:3-4
3 Then they came to Him, bringing a paralytic who was carried by four men. **4** And when they could not come near Him because of the crowd, they uncovered the roof where He was. So when they had broken through, they let down the bed on which the paralytic was lying.

That was their choice and they would not let anything or anyone get in their way of receiving a miracle of healing. Another example is found in

Mark 10:46-52
46 Now they came to Jericho. As He went out of Jericho with His disciples and a great multitude, blind Bartimaeus, the son of Timaeus, sat by the road begging. **47** And when he heard that it was Jesus of Nazareth, he began to cry out and say, "Jesus, Son of David, have mercy on me! **48** Then many warned him to be quiet; but he cried out all the more, Son of David, have mercy on me! **49** So Jesus stood still and commanded him to be called. Then they called the blind man, saying to him, Be of good cheer. Rise, He is calling you. **50** And throwing aside his garment, he rose and came to Jesus. **51** So Jesus answered and said to him, What do you want Me to do for you? The blind man said to Him, Rabboni, that I may receive my sight. **52** Then Jesus said to him, Go your way; your faith has made you well. And immediately he received his sight and followed Jesus on the road.

Here is Bartimaeus crying out to Jesus for mercy and the crowd began to tell him to be quiet, to hush up. Don't you know this is Jesus the Christ? He chose not to listen to the crowd, but to reach out in faith saying, **Jesus,** have mercy on me."

How many people do you know who will listen to their friends, family, and the crowd. "You don't want to go there. They're a bunch of tongue talkers. They believe in that faith stuff". Bartimaeus chose to go with what he believed. He believed in the power of Jesus. He had heard that "Jesus was going about doing good and healing all that were oppressed of the devil". You need to have the same bulldog tenacity and choose to believe in the healing power of God. Reach out with the hand of faith and say, "devil get your hands off my body". I plead the blood of Jesus over my body and by His stripes I am healed.

Notice in verse fifty-one that Jesus asked him what he wanted. Don't you think Jesus can see that the man was blind? Jesus wants us to come to Him and ask Him. That is showing Him that we are believing Him for our healing. We have faith in Him.

(3) Wavering will keep us from being healed.

> **James 1:5-8**
> **5** If any of you lacks wisdom, let him ask of God, who gives to all liberally and without reproach, and it will be given to him. **6** But let him ask in faith, with no doubting, for he who doubts is like a wave of the sea driven and tossed by the wind. **7** For let not that man suppose that he will receive anything from the Lord; **8** he is a double-minded man, unstable in all his ways.

In context, this is talking about wisdom. He says if we are wavering back and forth like the wave of the seas, we will not receive anything from the Lord and that includes healing. Verse eight says a double minded man is unstable. An unstable person will not receive anything from the Lord. The Word of God will make us become stable so that we can receive from the Lord.

As a pastor I have prayed for people to be saved, healed

and delivered. It is sad that no matter how much you pour into people the Word, there are those who will not grab hold of it. There are a few cases where some will say, "I don't feel saved", "I'm not saved because I don't feel it", or "I felt better when you prayed for me, but now I am hurting again. I don't know if God heard me or healed me". One day they're saved and healed and the next day they're not. That is what you call an unstable person.

The Bible says that this type of person will not receive anything from the Lord, that includes healing. No matter how much you fast and pray, if you keep swinging back and forth, one day you're healed and the next day you're not. You need to saturate yourself in the Word of God in the area of faith and healing scriptures. Romans10:17 "So then faith comes by hearing, and hearing by the word of God".

We need to keep hearing the Word of God over and over again to have it do a work in us. If I eat my greens once a year it will not do me any good. I need to eat my greens daily. You have to get the Word of God in you on a daily basis, just like eating your greens, for the Word to do any good.

(4) Some do not get healed because of the traditions of men.

Colossians. 2:8 "Beware lest anyone cheat you through philosophy and empty deceit, according to the **tradition of men**, according to the basic principles of the **world, and not according to Christ"**.

The traditions of men will kill you and keep you sick if you are not careful. Traditions come in many shapes or forms, such as, where you grew up, whether we are from the south, north, east, or west. Then there are your school, your work, your family, and even your church traditions. There are people who will say things like, "Bible or no Bible, this is where my great grandparents, my grandparents, and my parents went to church, and this is where I will go to

Church". Even if they're being taught wrong, people will stay there because it is comfortable for them. Here are a few more examples.

Tradition A: The teaching that sickness and disease brings more glory to God. This is absurd. It brings God more glory to see the devil rebuked and a person healed.

Tradition B: The day of miracles and healings are past. I like how F.F Bosworth puts this. "This is the most foolish, illogical, and unscriptural of any that I know".

> **Mark 16:17-18**
> **17** And these signs will follow those who believe: In My name they will cast out demons; they will speak with new tongues; **18** they will take up serpents; and if they drink anything deadly, it will by no means hurt them; they will lay hands on the sick, and they will recover.

Question: Are there anymore believers out there? If so, Jesus said in His name, we are to lay hands on the sick and they will recover.

Tradition C: Some don't receive their healing because they believe it's not God's will to heal all. I believe I have covered this quite well.

Tradition D: If it be Your will. The reason people use this is it puts all the responsibility on God and none on the person to receive healing. Their attitude is, "I don't have to change the way I am living. It's no big deal whether I am walking right with God, serving Him, giving tithes and offerings and doing my best to live a holy life". They think, so what!, if it's God's will for me to be healed, then I will. If not, it doesn't matter what I do; I won't be healed". No, that is a wrong attitude. We have a part to play in this. We need to bring our lives in line with the Word of God and do what

He tells us to do. If we do our part, He will do His part.

John 15:7 "If you abide in Me, and My Words abide in you, you will ask what you desire, and it shall be done for you". His Word needs to be abiding in us to work on our behalf.

You can tell whether the Word is abiding in someone when hard times hit. Out of the abundance of the heart the mouth speaks. If you're abiding in His Word, the healing Word will come out of you when you need it the most.

> **Deuteronomy 28:1-6**
> **1** Now it shall come to pass, **if you diligently obey the voice of the LORD** your God, to observe carefully all His commandments which I command you today, that the LORD your God will set you high above all nations of the earth. **2 And all these blessings** shall come upon you and overtake you, **because you obey the voice of the LORD** your God: **3** Blessed shall you be in the city, and blessed shall you be in the country. **4 Blessed shall be the fruit of your body**, the produce of your ground and the increase of your herds, the increase of your cattle and the offspring of your flocks. **5** Blessed shall be your basket and your kneading bowl. **6** Blessed shall you be when you come in, and blessed shall you be when you go out.

The fruit of your body will be blessed. That is talking about healing as well as your offspring. If you obey the Word of God, all these blessings will come upon you. "If" is the key word here.

Tradition E: Sickness is the will of God. If this is the case, then we should not go to Him and ask for healing. We would be going against His will. Wrong! He wants us to come to Him. James 5:14,15

Every person who goes to the doctors to get better is sinning and going against the will of God. That would also make all the doctors law breakers. Thank God for doctors. God gave them the technology that they know to help keep people alive.

(5) Why some do not receive their healing. Some are not healed because the one praying for them is not in faith and believing for a healing.

Matthew 18:9 "Again I say to you that if two of you agree on earth concerning anything that they ask, it will be done for them by My Father in heaven".

Sad to say, but not all believers believe in the healing power of God. Some believe, if it is His will, they will be healed. We need to be careful who we have agreeing with us. Make sure they believe the Word fully. They need to be in agreement with you and the Word of God.

(6) An unforgiving spirit.

> **Mark 11:25-26**
> **25** And whenever you stand praying, if you have anything against anyone, forgive him, that your Father in heaven may also forgive you your trespasses. **26** But if you do not forgive, neither will your Father in heaven forgive your trespasses.

We need to make sure that we are not holding a grudge or unforgiveness toward anyone-and I mean anyone. You know the one that God has been talking to you about and you keep wanting to put it aside. Resentment and unforgiveness will stop the flow of God's healing power in a heartbeat. We need to make sure that the pipeline is clear so God can do what we're asking of Him.

(7) Not being taught correctly about healing.
Some people think that healing is always instant, but it's not. That is a miracle. Healing can also take time. The reason why so many fail to receive is that they lose patience and give up. How long does it take for a broken bone to mend-or a skinned knee. The problem lies in the area of pain or some other thing that causes us to be immobile and we're looking to the outward signs of healing instead of looking at the Word. Hebrews 12:2 "Looking unto Jesus, the author and finisher of our faith, who for the joy that was set before Him endured the cross, despising the shame, and has sat down at the right hand of the throne of God".

Romans 4:19-21
19 And not being weak in faith, he did not consider his own body, already dead (since he was about a hundred years old), and the deadness of Sarah's womb. **20** He did not waver at the promise of God through unbelief, but was strengthened in faith, giving glory to God, **21** and being fully convinced that what He had promised He was also able to perform.

Notice it did not say that Abraham denied his body. It said he did not consider it. That means we are to acknowledge we are sick and need healing. Sometimes I think, some people keep their head stuck in the sand and deny every problem. He did not deny it; he just did not consider it. He was considering the promises of God instead of his dead body. He did not waver like so many people do today. It says he was strengthened in faith. How did he become strong in faith? By giving glory to God. As we continue to praise and worship Him through sickness and disease, He will strengthen us as well. Abraham was fully convinced that God will come through. We need to be just like Abraham and become fully convinced that God will heal our bodies.

(8) Some do not receive because of a lack of diligence.

Hebrews 11:6 "But without faith it is impossible to please Him, for he who comes to God must believe that He is, and that He is a rewarder of those who diligently seek Him". It says He is a rewarder to those who diligently seek Him. If we would only seek Him as much as we do other things. People seem to seek God only when they are in trouble. People are seeking their careers, sports, a spouse, fun and games, more than they are seeking God. They always have excuses, or they say, "Oh, I don't have time for church and all that church stuff. You could be missing out on a blessing. That same person has time to go to a football game for five hours on Sunday, but ask him to give two hours to God.

How much is your healing worth? Is it worth giving up the pleasures of life, like TV, sports and social activities to seek Him? Seek Him in the Word, in worship, and prayer and fasting, not just a minute or two a day, but spend hours seeking Him?

(9) Some fail to receive healing because they do not have the Word of God settled in their heart.

Proverbs 4:23 "Keep your heart with all diligence, for out of it spring the issues of life". The issues of life in this matter are health and healing. The reason it says to keep or (guard) your heart is because the Bible says "out of the abundance of the heart the mouth speaks". What we put in our hearts will come out during tests, trials, and tribulations. We need to cultivate our heart to make it good ground for the Word of God.

Luke 8:15 "But the ones that fell on the good ground are those who, having heard the word with a noble and good heart, keep it and bear fruit with patience". Just like a farmer tills the ground and makes it ready for planting, we are to till our heart with the Word, feed our heart the Word and we need to continue watering and fertilizing it. How do we water and fertilize our heart? With the Word of God.

Joshua 1:8
This Book of the Law shall not depart from your mouth, but you shall meditate in it day and night, that you may observe to do according to all that is written in it. For then you will make your way prosperous, and then you will have good success.

It says we are to meditate in the Word of God day and night, so that we would do the Word of God. And as we do the Word, then we can make our way prosperous and have good success. I do believe being totally healed is being prosperous in our body. Would you agree?

Psalms 1:1-3
1 Blessed is the man who walks not in the counsel of the ungodly, Nor stands in the path of sinners, Nor sits in the seat of the scornful; 2 But his delight is in the law of the LORD, and in His law he meditates day and night. 3 He shall be like a tree planted by the rivers of water, that brings forth its fruit in its season, whose leaf also shall not wither and whatever he does shall prosper.

In these scriptures the word "meditates" is used. The word "meditating" is better translated as mutter, speaking to yourself. It's like how a cow chews its cud. We are to keep chewing and chewing and chewing the Word of God until it brings a harvest. If we're not sowing the right seed in our hearts, we will not produce the right harvest.

Romans 10:8 "But what does it say? 'The word is near you, in your mouth and in your heart" (that is, the word of faith which we preach).

If I plant tomato seeds, what will I harvest? Tomatoes. If I plant carrot seeds, will I produce watermelons? Of course not! If I plant healing scriptures, what will I harvest? Healing. Keep planting healing scriptures and you will produce a harvest of healing. Philippians 1:6 "Being confident of this very thing, that He who has begun a good work in you will complete it until the day of Jesus Christ"; He started by saving you and delivering you from hell. Don't you think He wants to see you whole and healed.

(10) Some are not healed because they have no confidence in God and His will.

> **1 John 5:14-15**
> **14** Now this is the confidence that we have in Him, that if we ask anything according to His will, He hears us. **15** And if we know that He hears us, whatever we ask, we know that we have the petitions that we have asked of Him.

We have to know that He hears us when we pray. It is not enough to know that He hears pastor so and so, or sister so-and-so, or brother so-and-so, but that He hears us when we pray. Who is the us? You the reader of this book and anyone else who prays according to His will. As long as we are praying according to His will, and His will is for all to be healed, He hears us. If you know that He hears you when you pray according to His will, and His Word is His will, then you will have the petitions you asked of Him.

(11) Some are not healed because they would rather go to the doctors for a quick fix than to stand on the Word of God and wait for a manifestation of His healing power.

Let me explain what I mean. If someone is in serious pain and they had the choice of waiting on God or having surgery, they may choose surgery to get out of pain. Now that does not mean they have no faith. It means they want to be pain-free. Do not put people on a guilt trip or in condemnation if they have surgery. God has placed doctors here for us to use. Why not use them if need be?

This is just a partial list of why some do not receive their healing. The main thing is that God wants us healed. If someone does not get healed, it is not God's fault. Remember He is JEHOVAH-RAPHA-the Lord thy Physician. Exodus 15:26

CHAPTER TWELVE

What About Doctors?

One of the most misunderstood topics is medical science and the use of doctors. Some people think that if you use doctors, you are not in faith. Others will have you think that if you don't use doctors, you're in denial and being ignorant. Hopefully, this will help some of you. There is a balance in all things, including medical science and faith, for your healing. The Bible tells us to be specific in our prayers. How can we be specific if we do not know what to pray for? The only way we can know for sure what is wrong with us at times, is to go to the doctors so we can combat the issue in prayer.

Colossians 4:14 "Luke the beloved physician and Demas greet you".

Jesus called and picked all of His disciples. Why do you think Jesus picked Luke? He was a physician and He needed him on His team. If God did not want doctors here for us to use, He would not have given men the knowledge to be doctors. He gives to all of us the wisdom and understanding that we need to do what He has called us to do.

Under the Ministry of Jesus there was a woman who

went to doctors and wound up being healed by Jesus.

Mark 5:25-26
25 Now a certain woman had a flow of blood
for twelve years, **26** and had suffered many
things from many physicians. She had spent
all that she had and was no better, but rather
grew worse.

This shows that there were physicians back in those
days. Even though they did not help her, the fact remains the
same, there were doctors in Bible days. You may not be able
to be helped by a doctor, but at least you will know what to
pray for.

The doctor's back then did not know what they know
today and with the help of medical science today many
people are being helped.

I truly believe that God's way is the best way. However,
there are times we need those doctors to help. There is a
book on the market called "Faith, Foolishness, and
Presumption" by Fredrick KC Price. We need to know the
difference. Are we truly in faith, or are we afraid of what we
might hear from the doctors. It is foolish not to know what
we're up against. If I'm in pain, serious pain, I want to know
what it is. If it's cancer, a tumor, a blood disease or what, if I
know what it is then I know how to pray and what to ask for
in my prayers. The Word says to "ask and you shall
receive". Again, how can you ask for healing for something
when you don't know what it is?

I know people who have dealt with major depression
and I sent them to the doctors. They found out it was a
chemical imbalance in the brain. They started taking
medicine and are fine.

One thing about doctors, they are telling you the truth
from what they have been taught, but the truth of God's

Word is higher and better than their truth. Once you have their truth (and their truth may be, "there is no hope for you"), then you can thank them for the knowledge they gave and then go to prayer and know that God's Word is higher and better. Whose report will you believe? We shall believe the report of the Lord.

Now what about medication? Again, I have heard people say that if you're taking medication, you are not in faith. That is a lie from the pit of hell. First of all, medication does not heal anyone. It just covers up the problem, or fixes it temporarily.

There are people who will throw their medications or glasses away after hearing a message on faith and healing and after being prayed for. If after you hear a message on a topic of healing and are prayed for, do not throw your glasses away if you cannot see without them. You need them. You will know when you do not need your glasses. You will not be able to see with them on. The same goes for your medications.

So what about medication? Does wearing glasses heal your eyes? Does insulin heal diabetes? Does heart medication heal your heart? You get my point. None of these will heal you. They will take care of the symptoms, but they will not heal you.

Whether you are on medications or not, they have nothing to do with your healing. They cover up and take care of the symptoms and allow you to live fairly normal lives. You still need faith in God and His Word to heal you so you do not need those medications.

As you go to the doctors and take medications, keep trusting the Lord. Remember to say, "I believe I have received my healing when I prayed." That is a statement of faith and God will honor it. Some people would have you think that if you're taking medications, you're not healed, but, according to the Word, you are. You are just waiting for the manifestation of your healing as you confess the Word and do your part.

CHAPTER THIRTEEN

Healing Can Be Lost

"Divine healing is not "mental", as Christian Science, Unity, and other Metaphysical teachers claim. Neither is it physical, as the medical world teaches. When God heals, He heals through the spirit. God is not a mind. God is not a man. God is a Spirit. Being healed by the power of God is being healed by the Spirit of God. And because divine healing is spiritual, it can be lost. Many people have lost their healing by opening the door to the devil. (Kenneth E. Hagin Seven Things You Should Know About Divine Healing").

There are two main reasons why people lose their healing.

(1) Willful sin.

John 5:14 "Afterward Jesus found him in the temple, and said to him, "See, you have been made well. Sin no more, lest a worse thing come upon you."

This shows that sin was responsible for his sickness. Jesus said, "if he would continue in sin that this sickness may come back and even worse." We are not healed to live for the devil.

(2) Wavering faith.

1 Peter 5:9 "Resist him, steadfast in the faith, knowing that the same sufferings are experienced by your brotherhood in the world.

It says to resist the devil. We need to stand our ground and fight the good fight of faith. 1 Timothy 6:12

James 4:7-8 "Therefore submit to God. Resist the devil and he will flee from you". When we receive our healing, the devil will not give up. He will try to bring those old symptoms back on you and more. The scripture says to submit to God first, then you can resist the devil and he will flee from you. If you are not submitting your life to God (that includes your tongue-you know, the member of your body that speaks the Word of God, or death over your life), then you may be surprised that the devil does not have to flee from you.

Jesus has given us His authority by using the name of Jesus. To have authority we must be under authority; so if we're not submitted to God, the devil can have a hay-day with us. Remember, Satan is the god of this world. We are in his home so to speak, and he can throw at us anything he wishes, but we don't have to accept it.

2 Corinthians 4:3-4

Satan, who is the god of this evil world, has made him blind, unable to see the glorious light of the Gospel that is shining upon him or to understand the amazing message we preach about the glory of Christ, who is God. (TLB)

Ephesians 2:2-3
You went along with the crowd and were just
like all the others, full of sin, obeying Satan,
the mighty prince of the power of the air,
who is at work right now in the hearts of
those who are against the Lord. (TLB)

In these verses, we can see that Satan, the devil, is the
god of this world, but our God is bigger and greater. I said
all that to say this. If the devil tries to bring those old symptoms back, don't give in and say, "I guess I wasn't healed in
the first place". The moment you say that you are opening
the door to losing your healing.

We need to resist the devil and say, "I refuse to accept
that. You cannot put that back on me for I am healed. Those
are just lying symptoms and I refuse to take them in."

P.C. Nelson once said "More people lose their healing
over a counterattack than any other one thing." (Seven
Things You Should Know About Divine Healing), Kenneth
E. Hagin.

We need to learn and understand what the Bible says.
Believe it and confess it as final authority. Physical senses
will lie to us and try to keep us speaking what we feel
instead of what the Word of God says. We know we are
healed because we have been prayed for and we speak the
Word of God over our lives.

Matthew 8:17 "That it might be fulfilled which was
spoken by Isaiah the prophet, saying: **"He Himself took
our infirmities and bore our sicknesses."**

1 Peter 2:24 "Who Himself bore our sins in His own
body on the tree, that we, having died to sins, might live for
righteousness, **by whose stripes you were healed"**.

Isaiah 53:4-5
4 Surely He has borne our griefs and carried

our sorrows; Yet we esteemed Him stricken, Smitten by God, and afflicted. **5** But He was wounded for our transgressions, He was bruised for our iniquities; The chastisement for our peace was upon Him, And by His stripes we are healed.

How can anyone refute these scriptures. If God said it, it is true regardless of how we feel. When you get prayed over for healing and the person praying asks if you got it, are you healed, just say, "according to the Word of God and prayer, I believe I'm healed".

CHAPTER FOURTEEN

How to Keep Your Healing

If symptoms do come back, that does not mean that you were not healed in the first place. We are responsible for our willingness to cooperate with God's will or resist it. Keeping your healing means you have to yield to God's will. God is perfect and He only does perfect work. James 1:17 "Every good gift and every perfect gift is from above, and comes down from the Father of lights, with whom there is no variation or shadow of turning".

Since God can and will heal us, then it must be His will for us to stay healed. Would you as an earthly parent heal your child, then one day take the healing away? NO! I don't think you would. Well, how much more does our heavenly father want to do for us.

Matthew 7:11 "If you then, being evil, or (carnal) know how to give good gifts to your children, how much more will your Father who is in heaven give good things to those who ask Him"! Just take a moment and think about that. How do we keep our healing?

1. Stay in the realm of faith.

We need to hang out with those of like faith to build us up. People have called us at our church to meet with them and pray for healing for them. We would meet with these people and they would say, "oh, our Church doesn't believe like your Church does, so I would like you to pray for me". Then they would go right back to their doubting and unbelieving church. If your church does not believe as you do for healing, then you need a new church.

2. Stay in an attitude of praise and worship for your healing.

1 Thessalonians 5:18 "In everything give thanks; for this is the will of God in Christ Jesus for you". It doesn't say give thanks for your illness; it says in everything. In other words, giving Him praise that He is your healer. Praise is the gateway to your healing. Paul and Silas sang praises and God heard them and set them free.

Acts 16:25 "But at midnight Paul and Silas were praying and singing hymns to God, and the prisoners were listening to them".

Hebrews 13:15 "Through Him then, let us continually offer up a sacrifice of praise to God, that is, the fruit of lips that give thanks to His name". (NASU)

It is a sacrifice to praise God for our healing when we are racked with pain and sick with a fever. Sometimes that is the last thing on our mind, let alone what we feel like doing. But if we do praise and worship Him during this time, He will honor it by His healing power touching our bodies.

3. Keep telling people what God has done for you.

Revelations 12:11 "And they overcame him by the blood of the Lamb and by the word of their testimony, and they did not love their lives to the death". It says, "they overcame him (the devil)." We will overcome sickness and disease and counterattacks by His blood and our testimony. To have a testimony we need to go through a test.

We give praise reports and a time for testimonies in our church. This is a time not only for you to continue to be built up, but to build up one another's faith in God.

4. Feed your faith.

Just like we have to feed our body food to keep it alive, so we need to feed our spirit. Can you imagine eating one meal a week and being strong and fit enough to go water skiing, snow skiing, or hiking up a mountain. No!

And the same is true with our spirit man on the inside of us.

Romans 10:17 "So then faith comes by hearing, and hearing by the Word of God. If faith comes by hearing, then faith leaves by not hearing. We need to feed our faith with faith food (the Word of God). In Luke there is a story about Mary, Joseph, and Jesus going to Jerusalem for the feast of Passover. When the feast was over and they were on their way home, they were gone for three days and noticed that Jesus was not with them. So they back-tracked and found Him in the temple learning about the Word of God (feeding His spirit).

Luke 2:46 "Now so it was that after three days they found Him in the temple, sitting in the midst of the teachers, both listening to them and asking them questions".

Luke 2:52 "And Jesus increased in wisdom and stature, and in favor with God and men". As we feed ourselves the word, we become filled with the wisdom of God's Word and then it becomes like dynamite and explodes inside of us with His healing power.

Psalms 1:1-3

1 Blessed is the man Who walks not in the counsel of the ungodly, Nor stands in the path of sinners, Nor sits in the seat of the scornful; **2** But his delight is in the law of the LORD, And in His law he meditates day and night. **3** He shall be like a tree Planted by the rivers of water, That brings forth its fruit in its season, Whose leaf also shall not wither; And whatever he does shall prosper.

Verse two talks about meditating day and night. Someone will say, "I don't know how to meditate." We all meditate. It is a matter of what we're meditating on. When you keep going over in your mind with fear about a sickness, that is meditating. Why not meditate on the Word? It will bring forth fruit in the right season.

We all have a season. When your due season comes, it will bring forth healing in your body as you meditate on the Word, feeding your spirit.

5. Contend in faith for your healing.

1 Timothy 6:12 "Fight the good fight of faith, lay hold on eternal life, to which you were also called and have confessed the good confession in the presence of many witnesses". When the devil lies to you and says you're not healed, you need to give him an upper right cut. Knock his teeth out by speaking the Word of God. We are in the battle ring with the devil and he wants to win.

2 Corinthians 10:4-5

4 For the weapons of our warfare are not carnal but mighty in God for pulling down strongholds, **5** casting down arguments and every high thing that exalts itself against the knowledge of God, bringing every thought into captivity to the obedience of Christ.

As you can see, it says our warfare or boxing match. Yes, we are in a fight, but the verse in 1 Timothy 6:12 says it is a good fight. A good fight is one that you win, not lose. God sees you as the winner and not the loser. If He sees you as the winner then you need to see yourself as the winner, the overcomer, and the healed, in His name.

It goes on to say, "bringing every thought into captivity." When the devil comes telling your mind you're going under, you're going to be like this the rest of your life, that is the time to tell him, "no way". I am a born again child of God, a Christian-blood washed, healed and delivered. Take a firm stand on God's unfailing promises.

6. Walk in obedience to His Word, which is His will. Obedience always brings blessings on our life.

> **Deuteronomy 28:1-2**
> **1** Now it shall come to pass, if you diligently obey the voice of the LORD your God, to observe carefully all His commandments which I command you today, that the LORD your God will set you high above all nations of the earth. **2 And all these blessings shall come upon you and overtake you, because you obey the voice of the LORD your God:**

Why wouldn't anyone want to obey the Lord after reading this. Notice it says to observe His commandments. In the New Testament, the Lord has only one new commandment. John 13:34 "A new commandment I give to you, that you love one another; as I have loved you, that you also love one another". If we follow this one commandment, it will take care of the rest of them. Walking in love will bring the blessings of God into our lives; walking in love will keep us in obedience to the Word of God. That is why the devil always tries to get us into strife and division. To get us to walk out of love will keep us from the blessings of God. It opens the door for sickness and disease to come upon us. Let us make it a point to stay in the love walk.

CHAPTER FIFTEEN

The Healing Power Can Be In You and be Inactive

Rev. Kenneth E. Hagin will sometimes make a statement like this. "The moment I lay hands on you, the Healing Power of God will be administered to you. But what you do with it after that is up to you". (Understanding the Healing Power of God (Rev. Doug Jones).

"Just because the healing power is administered to your body does not guarantee that you will be healed". (Rev. Doug Jones, Understanding the Healing Power of God).

When I went to Bible School, I met a lot of people who said they were called to the Ministry. Since graduation there are quite of few that said they were called, but never stepped into the Ministry that God called them into. If they are not in the Ministry that God called them into, is the calling still on their life? Of course, they're just not doing what they were called to do. They chose a different life.

Romans 11:29 "For the gifts and the calling of God are irrevocable". This means that their calling is in them, but inactive.

Knowing this will help us understand that it is the same

way with the Healing Power of God. It can be in us and yet be inactive. I know this is new to some of you, but just stay with me on this one. It may set you free and cause the power that is in you to explode with healing.

1 Timothy 4:14 "Do not neglect the gift that is in you, which was given to you by prophecy with the laying on of the hands of the eldership."

> Neglect in the Greek is ameleo (am-el-eh'-o); from NT:1 (as a negative particle) and NT:3199; to be careless of: KJV - make light of, neglect, be negligent, no regard._

So we can have no regard and even be careless with the gift of healing in us. Paul is letting Timothy know that as a result of this neglected gift, it will not produce anything in or through Timothy's life until he does something with it.

We know this verse has nothing to do with healing, yet it does show the truth that we may have received something from having hands laid on us and it will do nothing unless we work it. God will not do the working of the Word Himself. We have to take the responsibility of our own actions and do something with the healing power of God that is to be active and working in us.

I have found out throughout the years that there are a lot of people who do not want to take responsibility for their own actions. Instead, they always blame someone or something for the condition or position they are in. God is not the one in charge of our life; we are.

2 Timothy 1:6 "Therefore I remind you to stir up the gift of God which is in you through the laying on of my hands." This is the second time that Paul reminds Timothy about this gift by having hands laid upon him. In both of these verses, it tells Timothy to do something with the gift, not God. We need to stir up and not neglect the gift of healing in us.

I will give you an example of what I am talking about. If I gave you a car as a gift, it is yours, not mine. You are the one to take care of it. If after driving it for quite some time you never change the oil, and you don't take care of it and the engine burns up, then you come to me and say, "hey what's the deal". I will turn around and say, "you were careless with the car". You ignored and neglected it. You should have taken care of what I gave you. It is the same way with healing. When you are prayed for and hands have been laid on you, it is your job to stir up the gift of healing that is in you.

The healing power of God will be in us, dormant, until we do something with it. It does not go away. If we don't do anything with the healing in us, then our sickness and disease will run our life until we decide to activate the Word and the healing power in us. It is the same way with walking the love walk. Romans 5:5 "Now hope does not disappoint, because the love of God has been poured out in our hearts by the Holy Spirit who was given to us." We all as born again Christians have the love of God in us, but until we decide to stir up that love, we can be as mean and ugly as the next person. It is in us, but we have to do something with it. It is called being a doer of the Word.

Sickness and disease will demand our attention, but what we put our attention on is what we will mostly stir up. We will give our attention to the symptoms or the Word of God. Most people will give more attention to the symptoms because that is what is most in front of them, the pain and all that we deal with. While it is easier to give into the symptoms than to stir up the Word of God, we must not neglect to stir up the healing power of God, which is in us.

There are a couple of ways to stir up the gift of healing in your body.

1 Timothy 4:14-15
14 Do not neglect the gift that is in you,

which was given to you by prophecy with the laying on of the hands of the eldership. **15** Meditate on these things; give yourself entirely to them, that your progress may be evident to all.

Meditation and giving yourself entirely will cause the gift to operate.

First, meditation: we all meditate. Some meditate on the problem, while others meditate on the Word of God. If you want real results, then think on the Word. Ponder the Word. Talk the Word, and give thanks about the Word of God and His healing power working in you.

Second is giving yourself entirely. This means being sold out. Nobody can talk you out of believing in the healing power of God living in you. Some people have given themselves entirely to sports. Look at those in the Olympics. They give themselves entirely to learning the sport they're in and it shows in those who get the gold. You do not become a world class skater just by watching them on TV. You put your all into it and then it is evident to all. That is what the Amplified says in verse 15-b "So that your progress may be evident to everybody." Whatever we behold, we become. If I give myself entirely to my job, I will climb the corporate ladder.

Don't quit! Your faith will see you through as you give yourself entirely to the Word of God and confess the healing scriptures over your life. There are a lot of people who start out with the right attitude and bulldog tenacity to get into the Olympics. Then they make it in, but they still need to keep training to get the gold. Have you ever noticed that there are three winners-the gold, the silver, and the bronze? Not every one gets the gold-only the best. The best gave it their all. They gave themselves entirely to the sport. They did not have much of a social life at all. There is too much at risk for you and me not to give ourselves completely and wholly to what will heal us.

Philippians 3:12-14

12 Not that I have already attained, or am already perfected; but I press on, that I may lay hold of that for which Christ Jesus has also laid hold of me. **13** Brethren, I do not count myself to have apprehended; but one thing I do, forgetting those things which are behind and reaching forward to those things which are ahead, **14** I press toward the goal for the prize of the upward call of God in Christ Jesus.

In verse fourteen, Paul is talking about pressing toward the goal. What is your goal? Your goal should be, to be completely healthy and whole and healed as God intended for you to be. I like how Brother Kenneth Copeland puts it. "We are the healed that the devil is trying to make sick." We are the healed!

The word "press" in this verse is NT: 1377 metaphorically, with the accusative of thing, to pursue, i. e. to seek after eagerly, earnestly endeavor to acquire: (from Thayer's Greek Lexicon). Let's earnestly endeavor to acquire our healing.

CHAPTER SIXTEEN

Does Sickness Glorify God?

Everywhere you go in this world there are sick people, both Christian and non-Christian. The sad thing about it is, there are too many people sick in the church today. Sickness and disease will hit all people in all walks of life. The rich and the poor, the White, the Black, the Hispanic, the American Indian, yellow or green, it does not matter. You name it and it will hit. Sickness and disease are no respecter of persons.

Down through the ages people have said, "Well, this can be a blessing in disguise." Show me that in the Bible. Or you will hear people say, "this sickness is for God's glory." Oh, is it? Does God really get glory out of us being sick and afflicted with disease? I ask you, would you get glory out of putting cancer on your child or parents? I can not imagine God up in heaven, jumping up and down, saying, "I'm so happy and thrilled that so and so has a disease. That is just great, cool, that makes me happy." No! That is plain ignorant and dumb.

What are you basing your opinion on. Is it on whether or not God gets glory out of us being sick by what someone

said, or what the Bible says? You will have to show me
chapter and verse in the bible for me to accept that God gets
glory out of His people being sick. It's not in there.

Some teach that God does get glory from us being sick,
but that is because they got frustrated and gave up on being
healed. It came from their mind and not the Word of God.
So let's look at the Word of God.

Acts 10:38
How God anointed and consecrated Jesus of
Nazareth with the (Holy) Spirit and with
strength and ability and power; how He
went about doing good and, in particular,
curing all who were harassed and oppressed
by (the power of) the devil, for God was
with Him. (Amplified Bible).

It says Jesus went about doing good. Being healed is a
good thing. Why would God heal all and then turn around
and make people sick? It does not compute. Notice also, it
says curing **all.** All means all-not one or two or a handful, but
all who were oppressed by the devil. Sickness and disease is
Satanic oppression. I did not say you are possessed; I said
oppressed.

Oppression means (1) (A) "an unjust or
cruel exercise of authority or power, (B)
something that oppress esp. in being an
unjust or excessive exercise of power (2) a
sense of being weighed down in body or
mind. Depression". (Webster's Ninth New
Collegiate Dictionary).

Number two of the meaning of oppression says, "Being
weighed down in body." That is what oppression is. Sickness

and disease is an oppression that weighs a person down. It keeps you from enjoying the pleasures of life, going about your daily duties, keeping a job, having peace and joy in your family. Some people can not even do what most people take for granted like bowling, hiking, skating, and so on. Does that really sound like a loving God to you? Do you think God gets joy or glory when His children can not enjoy life the way He wants us to?

Luke 13:10-16

10 Now He was teaching in one of the synagogues on the Sabbath. **11** And behold, there was a woman who had a spirit of infirmity eighteen years, and was bent over and could in no way raise herself up. (I wonder if God got Glory and joy out of that) **12** But when Jesus saw her, He called her to Him and said to her, Woman, you are loosed from your infirmity. **13** And He laid His hands on her, and immediately she was made straight, and glorified God.(do you see that God got glory when we was made whole) **14** But the ruler of the synagogue answered with indignation, because Jesus had healed on the Sabbath; and he said to the crowd, There are six days on which men ought to work; therefore come and be healed on them, and not on the Sabbath day. **15** The Lord then answered him and said, Hypocrite! Does not each one of you on the Sabbath loose his ox or donkey from the stall, and lead it away to water it? **16** So ought not this woman, being a daughter of Abraham, whom Satan has bound (think of it) for eighteen years, be loosed from this bond on the Sabbath?

It says, that Satan had bound her, not God. It does not take much to figure this out. People will tell you God brings sickness on people. That is not what this says. Look at when God got the glory after she was healed. It says she had an **infirmity** from the devil. Infirmity is a spirit and in this case it is an evil spirit. The Word says Satan had bound her. This type of infirmity will cause a person to be bent over, weak, feeble, frail, in mind and body.

Matthew 9:1-8
1 So He got into a boat, crossed over, and came to His own city. **2** Then behold, they brought to Him a paralytic lying on a bed. When Jesus saw their faith, He said to the paralytic, Son, be of good cheer; your sins are forgiven you. **3** And at once some of the scribes said within themselves, "This Man blasphemes! **4** But Jesus, knowing their thoughts, said, Why do you think evil in your hearts? **5** For which is easier, to say, Your sins are forgiven you, or to say, Arise and walk? **6** But that you may know that the Son of Man has power on earth to forgive sins then He said to the paralytic, Arise, take up your bed, and go to your house. **7** And he arose and departed to his house. **8** Now when the multitudes saw it, they marveled and glorified God, who had given such power to me.

There is no mention in these verses that says while this man was on his sick bed that God got any glory from him. But when he received his healing and picked up his bed and walked away, the crowd began to give God glory. In this case, God got all the glory when the man got healed, not when he was sick.

Matthew 15:29-31

29 Jesus departed from there, skirted the Sea of Galilee, and went up on the mountain and sat down there. **30** Then great multitudes came to Him, having with them the lame, blind, mute, maimed, and many others; and they laid them down at Jesus' feet, and He healed them. **31** So the multitude marveled when they saw the mute speaking, the maimed made whole, the lame walking, and the blind seeing; and they glorified the God of Israel.

When did God get the glory? When the people got healed. Look at it yourself. God did not get any glory from the people when they were bound and sick. They didn't walk around and say, "thank God that I can't see, or hear, or walk." No! They gave Him glory for the healing.

Luke 17:11-19

11 Now it happened as He went to Jerusalem that He passed through the midst of Samaria and Galilee. **12** Then as He entered a certain village, there met Him ten men who were lepers, who stood afar off. **13** And they lifted up their voices and said, Jesus, Master, have mercy on us! **14** So when He saw them, He said to them, Go, show yourselves to the priests. And so it was that as they went, they were cleansed. **15** And one of them, when he saw that he was healed, returned, and with a loud voice glorified God, **16** and fell down on his face at His feet, giving Him thanks. And he was a Samaritan. **17** So Jesus answered and said, Were there not ten cleansed? But where are the nine? **18** Were there not any found who returned to give glory to God except this foreigner? **19** And He said to him, Arise, go your way. Your faith has made you well.

Back then, when a person had leprosy and they were not allowed to be around other people, if someone came near them they were to yell out, "**UNCLEAN, UNCLEAN**". The reason for this was to let others know that there were lepers close by. After a person was healed of leprosy, they were to go show themselves to the priest to be certified that they were healed. Notice Jesus told them to go show themselves clean to the priest before they were clean. And as they went they were cleansed. That is faith. We need to act on the Word just like they did. Verse fifteen says that only one came back to give God glory for his healing. Again, when did God get the glory? After the healing. And then Jesus said of the man that had leprosy, that his faith healed him.

Acts 3:1-8
1 Now Peter and John went up together to the temple at the hour of prayer, the ninth hour. **2** And a certain man lame from his mother's womb was carried, whom they laid daily at the gate of the temple which is called Beautiful, to ask alms from those who entered the temple; **3** who, seeing Peter and John about to go into the temple, asked for alms. **4** And fixing his eyes on him, with John, Peter said, Look at us. **5** So he gave them his attention, expecting to receive something from them. **6** Then Peter said, "Silver and gold I do not have, but what I do have I give you: In the name of Jesus Christ

of Nazareth, rise up and walk." **7** And he took him by the right hand and lifted him up, and immediately his feet and ankle bones received strength. **8** So he, leaping up, stood and walked and entered the temple with them, walking, leaping, and praising God.

What was the lame man doing when Peter and John saw him? Was he praising God and giving God glory? NO! He was asking for alms and begging. He most likely had some kind of cup to receive alms. He was saying things like, "I can't work; I can't hold a job; I'm poor; will you help me."

Praise God! When that man was healed, the Bible says that he "**LEAPED UP AND STOOD AND WALKED, LEAPING AND PRAISING GOD**". Verse eight, he wasn't begging anymore. He was giving God glory for the healing power of God working in him.

Luke 18:35-43

35 Then it happened, as He was coming near Jericho, that a certain blind man sat by the road begging. **36** And hearing a multitude passing by, he asked what it meant. **37** So they told him that Jesus of Nazareth was passing by. **38** And he cried out, saying, "Jesus, Son of David, have mercy on me!" **39** Then those who went before warned him that he should be quiet; but he cried out all the more, "Son of David, have mercy on me!" **40** So Jesus stood still and commanded him to be brought to Him. And when he had come near, He asked him, **41** saying, "What do you want Me to do for you?" And he said, "Lord, that I may receive my sight." **42** Then Jesus said to him, "Receive your sight; your faith has made you well." **43** And immediately he received his sight, and followed Him, glorifying God. And all the people, when they saw it, gave praise to God.

This man was persistent. He cried out to Jesus. Those who went before him told this poor blind man to be quiet and to mind his own business, but he cried out even more, "SON OF DAVID HAVE MERCY ON ME!" He would not listen to the people. Do you know that a lot of people will give in to peer pressure? You don't want to go to that church do you? Why they believe in speaking in tongues, laying hands on the sick and getting them healed, casting out demons. Well, if you want your healing enough you will say yes, yes, I want to go there and learn the Word and be healed. Don't give into the pressures of people. Do what the Word says.

Notice again in verse forty-one, Jesus asked him what he wanted. Jesus can see the man was blind, and He said, "what do you want." The Father, Son, and the Holy Spirit, plus the Word of God will always want us to ask. Even though God knows what you need, He wants us to ask. Then the man said, "I want to receive my sight." So Jesus said, "receive your sight; your faith has made you well." Jesus didn't even lay hands on him. Notice it was the blind man's faith that made him well. It was his faith in the Healing Power of Jesus Christ.

In verse forty-three, it says, "when he received his sight he gave glory to God and all the people including the sinners around gave glory and praise to God as well."

Nowhere in this scripture does it say they were giving God glory while the man was blind. They were telling him to be quiet and mind his own business and leave the master alone.

Luke 7:11-16

11 Now it happened, the day after, that He went into a city called Nain; and many of His disciples went with Him, and a large crowd. **12** And when He came near the gate of the city, behold, a dead man was being carried out, the only son of his mother; and she was a widow. And a large crowd from the city was with her. **13** When the Lord saw her, He had compassion on her and said to her, "Do not weep." **14** Then He came and touched the open coffin, and those who carried him stood still. And He said, "Young man, I say to you, arise." **15** So he who was dead sat up and began to speak. And He presented him to his mother. **16** Then fear came upon all, and they glorified God, saying, "A great prophet has risen up among us"; and, "God has visited His people."

Verse thirteen says Jesus had compassion on this woman who lost her son. God the Father and Jesus the Son have so much compassion for the sick that they want to see the sick healed more than those who are sick. In verse sixteen, it shows that, after the boy came back to life, fear came upon all those who were around and they began to glorify God. It says all the people, believer and non- believer, gave God glory. Was there glory in his death, or in his coming back to life?

John 9:1-7

1 Now as Jesus passed by, He saw a man who was blind from birth. **2** And His disciples asked Him, saying, "Rabbi, who sinned, this man or his parents, that he was born blind?" **3** Jesus answered, "Neither this man nor his parents sinned, but that the works of God should be revealed in him. **4** I must work the works of Him who sent Me while it is day; the night is coming when no one can work. **5** As long as I am in the world, I am the light of the world." **6** When He had said these things, He spat on the ground and made clay with the saliva; and He anointed the eyes of the blind man with the clay. **7** And He said to him, "Go, wash in the pool of Siloam" (which is translated, Sent). So he went and washed, and came back seeing.

Notice the disciples asked Jesus, who sinned, that this man was born blind- His parents or himself. We all know that a person cannot sin while in the womb of the mother (at least I haven't seen or heard of it). For some reason, the Jews thought that you can sin while in your mother's womb. Well we know better than that.

Jesus gives them their answer. Neither sinned, but that the works of God may be revealed in him. Some translations say,

"but to show what God could do in his case" Williams Translation, "It was to let Gods work be shown plainly in him" The New Testament: "New Translation" (Olaf M. Norlie), "but to show the power of God at work in him" The New Testament in Modern English.

It did not say for God to get any kind of glory from him being born blind. Nor did it say that the work of God was that the man be blind. If that was the case, Jesus violated His Father's works because He healed the man. No! It was to show the power of God at work in him. Jesus said, "I came to do the Father's work." Part of His work is healing. Remember what the scripture says. God anointed Jesus Christ with the Holy Spirit and power, who went about doing good and healing all.

Is God glorified through sickness and disease? No! He is not. Common sense tells us, if there were scriptures that showed us God was glorified through sickness, it would contradict what I have shown you already. And that, my friend, will not happen. Remember, "He is the same yesterday, today and forever". He changes not.

CHAPTER SEVENTEEN

The Suffering Christian

Isaiah 55:9 "For as the heavens are higher than the earth, So are My ways higher than your ways, And My thoughts than your thoughts."

God's ways and thoughts are much, much higher than ours. We need to come up to His way of thinking. We need to climb up out of the pit, thinking that we are just suffering for the Lord. Are we just suffering for the Lord or are we just ignorant of the truth of His word? I submit to you that we have been brain-washed instead of scripturally taught. Yes, but didn't Jesus say He was perfected by His suffering? Yes, He did. But was it through sickness and disease? Or something else.

Hebrews 5:8-9 "Though He was a Son, yet He learned obedience by the things which He suffered. And having been perfected, He became the author of eternal salvation to all who obey Him."

People all around the world who are dealing with some kind of sickness and disease will try to convince you they are suffering for Jesus. They're suffering, all right, but not for Jesus. It is because of a lack of teaching on the area of healing.

1 Peter 2:9-19

9 But you are a chosen generation, a royal priesthood, a holy nation, His own special people, that you may proclaim the praises of Him who called you out of darkness into His marvelous light; **10** who once were not a people but are now the people of God, who had not obtained mercy but now have obtained mercy. **11** Beloved, I beg you as sojourners and pilgrims, abstain from fleshly lusts which war against the soul, **12** having your conduct honorable among the Gentiles, that when they speak against you as evildoers, they may, by your good works which they observe, glorify God in the day of visitation. **13** Therefore submit yourselves to every ordinance of man for the Lord's sake, whether to the king as supreme, **14** or to governors, as to those who are sent by him for the punishment of evildoers and for the praise of those who do good. **15** For this is the will of God, that by doing good you may put to silence the ignorance of foolish men— **16** as free, yet not using liberty as a cloak for vice, but as bondservants of God. **17** Honor all people. Love the brotherhood. Fear God. Honor the king. **18** Servants, be submissive to your masters with all fear, not only to the good and gentle, but also to the harsh. **19** For this is commendable, if because of conscience toward God one endures grief, suffering wrongfully.

Look at verse nineteen. It says endure grief, suffering wrongfully. This is not talking about sickness or disease. We do not need to suffer with sickness and disease because we have been washed by the blood of Jesus. He took stripes upon His back for our healing and we are redeemed from all that. Now the Bible does talk about suffering wrongfully. So what does that mean?

1 Peter 2:20-21
20 For what credit is it if, when you are beaten for your faults, you take it patiently? But when you do good and suffer, if you take it patiently, this is commendable before God. **21** For to this you were called, because Christ also suffered for us, leaving us an example, that you should follow His steps:

There is a difference in Jesus Christ's example in suffering and His substitution of suffering. We can follow His example in suffering, as a Christian, a follower of Him, believing in healing, tongues, and the gifts of the Spirit, but not in His substitution because in that, He was taking our place. He left us an example to follow.

1 Peter 2:22-23
22 "Who committed no sin, Nor was deceit found in His mouth"; **23** who, when He was reviled, did not revile in return; when He suffered, He did not threaten, but committed Himself to Him who judges righteously;

Verse twenty-three says He suffered. How did He suffer? In persecutions. He suffered by claiming He was the Christ, the Son of the Living God. He suffered because He healed on the Sabbath. He suffered because He brought a New Commandment to live by. He suffered because He walked what He taught. He was giving instructions on how to live a Godly and holy life, which, like today, even back then people did not want to hear.

In His suffering on the cross, shedding His blood for us and taking our sins, sickness and disease upon Himself, He was our Substitute. He did suffer on the cross. Do you remember the Scripture in the garden of Gethsemane when He knew He was going to the cross? With tears as great drops of blood coming out of Him, He asked the Father, "if this cup could pass from me". Then He said "nevertheless, not my will but yours be done". That's suffering, my friend. How many people do you know who would die on the cross for your sickness and disease? Praise God, He sent His Son to take our place, shed His blood and took stripes on His back, so we can receive His healing into our bodies.

Hebrews 2:18 "For in that He Himself has **suffered, being tempted**, He is able to aid those who are tempted." He suffered temptation just like you and I do, but passed the tests of those temptations.

Hebrews 4:15 "For we do not have a High Priest who cannot sympathize with our weaknesses, but was in all points **tempted** as we are, yet without sin."

I have been sharing about Jesus. What about the Apostles? What did they suffer from? Acts 5:41 "So they departed from the presence of the council, rejoicing that they were counted worthy to suffer shame for His name."

Peter and John were beaten and told not to teach people about Jesus. I call that suffering in the name of the Lord, don't you? We have it really good in our country. We can speak and teach all about Jesus without being beaten or stoned.

As you can see, even back in what is called Bible days, people were beaten and stoned for the preaching of the cross. From 1999 and well into the year 2000, my mother-in-law spent a year in the Holy Lands. After she came home, she told us that she had stones thrown at her for witnessing on the streets. I call that suffering for the cause of the Lord.

Now Peter and John were rejoicing that they were suffering shame for the sake of preaching Jesus.

Acts 9:10-16

10 Now there was a certain disciple at Damascus named Ananias; and to him the Lord said in a vision, "Ananias." And he said, "Here I am, Lord." **11** So the Lord said to him, "Arise and go to the street called Straight, and inquire at the house of Judas for one called Saul of Tarsus, for behold, he is praying. **12** And in a vision he has seen a man named Ananias coming in and putting his hand on him, so that he might receive his sight." **13** Then Ananias answered, "Lord, I have heard from many about this man, how much harm he has done to Your saints in Jerusalem. **14** And here he has authority from the chief priests to bind all who call on Your name." **15** But the Lord said to him, "Go, for he is a chosen vessel of Mine to bear My name before Gentiles, kings, and the children of Israel. **16** For I will show him how many things he must suffer for My name's sake."

In verse sixteen, Jesus said, "Paul will suffer many things for Jesus name sake." Paul did not suffer in sickness and disease like a lot of people would have you believe. So in what did he suffer?

2 Corinthians 6:4-6

4 But in all things we commend ourselves as

ministers of God: in much patience, in **tribu-lations**, in needs, in distresses, **5** in stripes, in imprisonments, in tumults, in labors, in sleeplessness, in fastings; **6** by purity, by knowledge, by longsuffering, by kindness, by the Holy Spirit, by sincere love,

Verse four says tribulations. In the (KJV) it is the word afflictions, which is translated from the Strong's Concordance as pressure, (literally or figuratively): KJV afflicted, anguish, burdened, persecution, tribulation, and trouble.

2 Corinthians 11:23-31
23 Are they ministers of Christ? I speak as a fool, I am more: in labors more abundant, in stripes above measure, in prisons more frequently, in deaths often. **24** From the Jews five times I received forty stripes minus one. **25** Three times I was beaten with rods; once I was stoned; three times I was shipwrecked; a night and a day I have been in the deep; **26** in journeys often, in perils of waters, in perils of robbers, in perils of my own countrymen, in perils of the Gentiles, in perils in the city, in perils in the wilderness, in perils in the sea, in perils among false brethren; **27** in weariness and toil, in sleeplessness often, in hunger and thirst, in fastings often, in cold and nakedness, **28** besides the other things, what comes upon me daily: my deep concern for all the churches. **29** Who is weak, and I am not weak? Who is made to stumble, and I do not burn with indignation? **30** If I must boast, I will boast in the things which

concern my infirmity. **31** The God and Father of our Lord Jesus Christ, who is blessed forever, knows that I am not lying.

Vines Expository Dictionary of New Testament Words says that the word "infirmity" in verse thirty is the word "weakness" and rightly so. I guess I would be weak after all the tests, trials, and tribulations he went through. Is there anything in there that shows he was suffering sickness and disease?

Romans 8:17: "and if children, then heirs, heirs of God and joint heirs with Christ, if indeed we suffer with Him, that we may also be glorified together."

This word "suffer" is the pain of persecution as a follower of Jesus Christ. How many of you get persecuted for being a Christian?

Romans 8:18 "For I consider that the sufferings of this present time are not worthy to be compared with the glory, which shall be revealed in us."

As I mentioned earlier that my mother-in-law spent a year in the Holy Lands, she told me of how people suffer for talking about Jesus. We in this country really do not know what suffering persecution is really like. Paul is not talking about some disease, but living for the Lord and being a true follower of Him.

2 Corinthians 4:8-9 "We are hard pressed on every side, yet not crushed; we are perplexed, but not in despair; persecuted, but not forsaken; struck down, but not destroyed." Some dear people will use this scripture and tell you that sickness and disease just goes with being a Christian. They will say, "brother, I am hard pressed with cancer. I'm suffering for Jesus, but I will overcome. "They're just blinded from the truth".

1 Peter 5:10 "But may the God of all grace, who called us to His eternal glory by Christ Jesus, after you have suffered a

while, perfect, establish, strengthen, and settle you."

Suffering will cause us to grow up in the Lord if we allow the Holy Spirit to do a work in us. I have tried to show you that we are not to suffer with sickness and disease for the glory of God. God does not get any glory out of us being sick.

Some people suffer because they have no common sense. I found out common sense is not so common. For example, if it is forty-two degrees outside and raining, someone might go to the gym and work out. After they are done, they might not put on a jacket to go out in the cold, wet weather. If they catch a cold, whose fault is it?

Some will say the devil put this cold on them; others will say God is trying to teach them a lesson. The truth of the matter is, they were not using their brain.

We will suffer persecution living in a certain area, driving a certain car, wearing certain clothes, having too much money, and living by a certain set of beliefs in the Word of God. There is nowhere in the Bible that it talks about us suffering with sickness and disease for being a Christian, for the Glory of God.

John 16:33 "These things I have spoken to you, that in Me you may have peace. In the world you will have tribulation; but be of good cheer, I have overcome the world." God never promised us smooth sailing, just a safe landing.

And He has never said life would be a bed of roses.

CHAPTER EIGHTEEN

Trusting in a Faithful God

If you told your children on Monday that you were going to take them to the movies on Saturday and they came to you on Tuesday, Wednesday, and Thursday bugging you if you were going to take them, you would get upset, because you had already promised them that you would. You see by their actions, they are letting you know that they doubt your word. In much the same way, that is what we do with Jesus our Healer when we end our prayers with "if it be your will". The Bible is His will for us and it has been given to us, "with His stripes we are healed".

Romans 8:11 "But if the Spirit of Him who raised Jesus from the dead dwells in you, He who raised Christ from the dead will also give life to your mortal bodies through His Spirit who dwells in you."

The word "life" is the word quicken in the (KJV). The word quicken is NT:222 zoopoieo (dzo-op-oy-eh'-o); from the same as NT:2226 and NT:4160; to (re-) vitalize (literally or figuratively): It is also translated make alive, give life, and quicken.

Quite often our bodies need to be revitalized from being sick. He will give life to the members of your body that need to be touched. Maybe your liver is bad, or your heart or lungs. We need to speak life to them.

God is a faithful God. We all know some people who we cannot count on if our lives depended upon it. It used to be, a person's word could be trusted, but not so in a lot of people. God is not like that. He said what He meant and He meant what He said and He is faithful.

Numbers 23:19 "God is not a man, that He should lie, Nor a son of man, that He should repent. Has He said, and will He not do? Or has He spoken, and will He not make it good?"

The Lord will make it good in your life. He is not like people who say one thing and do another. If He said He has healed your body, then He has healed your body. Trust and believe in His Holy written Word. He is faithful and He will perform His Word in your life.

Isaiah 25:1 "O LORD, You are my God. I will exalt You, I will praise Your name, For You have done wonderful things; Your counsels of old are faithfulness and truth."

Look in your past and see how many times God has come through for you or someone else. That was the mistake the children of Israel made. Here was Moses being used by God to deliver them and set them free. They had seen the hand of God move in many ways, but then they came to the Red Sea and thought it was a dead end. Where are they going now? Then they looked back and saw Pharaoh and his army closing in and the children of Israel were ready to give up and die. Then God spoke to Moses and told him to stretch out his staff across the Red Sea. We all know the story of how God parted the Red Sea for them to cross over and when Pharaoh's army tried crossing the

Red Sea, God closed it up. The whole army died.

Hebrews10:23 "Let us hold fast the confession of our hope without wavering, for He who promised is faithful." Our confession is always to be, "I believe I have received my healing because by His stripes I am healed". If we hold to our confession then He will be faithful to watch over His word to perform it in our lives. We need to give Him something to work with, which is our faith confession. We need to be like Sarah, judging Him faithful.

Hebrews 11:11 "By faith Sarah herself also received strength to conceive seed, and she bore a child when she was past the age, because **she judged Him faithful who had promised."**

When we start judging God faithful because "He is not a man, that He should lie, nor a son of man, that He should repent", we have the same promise.

John 10:10 "The thief does not come except to steal, and to kill, and to destroy. I have come that they may have life, and that they may have it more abundantly."

Satan wants to steal your healing and destroy you with all kinds of sickness and disease, but Jesus said that He came to give us abundant life. Again, if we look to Him and judge Him faithful, then just as He did for all the Patriarchs in the Hall of Faith of Hebrews eleven, He will do for you.

CHAPTER NINETEEN

Keeping Your Mind on God's Word

Have you ever been in a situation, in a crowd of people, where you were trying to concentrate on a certain topic and you could not because of all the noise around you. The same thing is true when it comes to our healing. When our bodies are screaming at us, sometimes it takes everything in us to concentrate on God's Word. No matter how hard it is, we will benefit from it.

Isaiah 26:3 "You will keep him in perfect peace, Whose mind is stayed on You, Because he trusts in You." If we are truly trusting Him for our healing, then our minds will stay on Him and His healing Word. When we spend time in the Word, trusting and believing Him, then and only then will we stay in perfect peace. That is true faith. Because you are trusting in the healing power of the Word of God, instead of how your body feels, then He will keep you in peace because your mind is on Him.

It is like going to the doctor. The doctor gives you a prescription to take a certain pill three times a day for four weeks. You would follow that prescription if you want the best results. God's medicine works the same way. His Word is your daily prescription and it is as follows:

> **Proverbs 4:20-23**
> **20** My son, give attention to my words; Incline your ear to my sayings. **21** Do not let them depart from your eyes; Keep them in the midst of your heart; **22** For they are life to those who find them, And health to all their flesh. **23** Keep your heart with all diligence, For out of it spring the issues of life.

First, it says to give attention to His Word.

This means putting His Word first and foremost in your life. Successful people do not become successful without paying attention to what they are striving for. Take a lawyer or doctor, for example. Look at all the school years and the study time they have to put in to get where they want to be. Most of the time, they don't even have time for a social life because they are giving all their time and attention to their study and learning for their career.

If we give our full attention to God's Word-study, learn, and meditate-then we will see the fruit of it taking place in our lives. Jesus said "out of the abundance (or overflow) of the heart the mouth speaks." When we give our full attention to God's Word, our minds will be clear and sharp as a tack. So all that will come out of our mouth is His Word and not doubt and fear or what the doctors say.

Second, it says to incline your ear to His sayings.

Incline means to bend the head or body forward, to lean, tend, or become drawn toward an opinion or course of conduct. Incline implies a tendency to favor one of two or more actions or conclusions. (Webster's Ninth New Collegiate Dictionary.)

Simply put, we are to be drawn and lean into the Word of God and favor what His Word has to say about our condition. By the Word of God, we will come to a conclusion that it is His will for us to be healed. We are to go after God's Word because it is a matter of life and death to us. Some people will call in sick to their job to go to a sports event. That is what we call inclining to the sports.

While there are good conferences and meetings to go to, people can come up with a million excuses why they cannot make church or a conference. They are inclining to the wrong thing. If they need God to do something in their life and they are not seeking and listening to the Word of God then they are deceiving themselves.

Every chance I get, I go to different meetings to get filled up with the Word and sit under the anointing of the Holy Spirit. That is the only thing that will help me in this life. We need to be a "Word and anointing chaser". Don't just wait for a special meeting in your church, or in your town. Seek one out and go to one. Even if you have to fly out of state, it will be worth it. We need to have more desire for His Word than anything else. Always remember this, "You become what you behold or you become what you incline yourself to."

Third, it says "let them not depart from your eyes".

Train your eyes to stay on the Word and not on your circumstances. It is much like playing Ping-Pong or shooting pool or playing baseball. We have to keep our eyes on the ball if we want to hit it. We need to keep the Word in front of our eyes and look at the Word instead of what we are going through. That is what Abraham did. In Romans it says that he did not consider his body, but considered the promises of God instead. In other words, he kept the promise of God's Word in front of his eyes. Your eyes and ears are the gateway to your heart. Whatever you put before you is going to take root and come out of you.

Attend to His word; incline your ear to His sayings; and do not let them depart from your eyes.

Fourth, "keep them (His Word) in the midst of your heart."

Just like natural food keeps us alive, so it is with spiritual food from the Word of God. In Hebrews 4:12 it states that the Word of God is "living and powerful". The Word of God is alive and active when we put it in our spirit man. It does not do you any good to have your Bible setting on the shelf collecting dust. The Word put in our spirit mixed with faith causes it to become powerful and active in us. The Word works when we work it in our spirit man. If you stopped eating for no reason at all, you just felt like not eating for a week or two, how strong would your body feel? Will you feel like running a marathon race? I don't think so. The same is true with our spirit man. We need to continue to feed it the Word of God in order for our spirit man to be strong and walk in divine health and healing. The Bible says that, "faith comes by hearing, and hearing by the Word of God". Just because you heard a message on healing last month does not mean you have it. You need to read and listen to teachings on healing as much as possible. The Thanksgiving dinner I had last year does not satisfy me forever. In fact, I would like to have the same dinner more often, but it is a lot of work. Don't just expect a message you heard last year to help you out. Chances are you have forgotten a lot of it. They do not call them refresher courses for no reason at all. We need to be refreshed in what we have been taught.

Fifth, "for they (the Word of God) are life to those who find them, and health to all their flesh".

The Word of God or God's Word are spirit and they are

also life. (John 6:33) The Word of God is life, health, and medicine to all that find them. That means we have to dig it out like it was gold.

The word "life" comes from the Greek word "Zoe" meaning life (literally or figuratively): and the word "spirit" comes from the Greek word "pneuma" meaning a current of air, breath, (blast) or a breeze; The Holy Spirit will blast a current of air into your body and breath zoe or life into you. This is what will happen as a result of keeping the Word of God in front of us and not letting it depart from our eyes. If we will make the time to attend to His Word, we shall be blessed. We seem to make time to attend to our favorite show or game. So take time to attend to the Word of God because it is health to all your flesh.

The word "health" is the Hebrew word

> marpe' (mar-pay'); from OT:7495; properly, curative, i.e. literally (concretely) a medicine, or (abstractly) a cure; figuratively (concretely) deliverance, or (abstractly) placidity: (KJV) - (in) cure (able), healing (the), remedy, sound, wholesome, yielding.

So we can put it this way, that God's Word is health, medicine, a cure, deliverance and healing for our bodies. You won't find that in a doctor's office.

Sixth, keep your heart with all diligence.

The Hebrew word for "keep" is "natsar", to guard in a good sense, to protect and maintain. We are to put a guard around our heart and protect it from the pollution of the world of doubt and unbelief. Some people, even though they mean well, will fill your heart with all kinds of doubt, saying things like, "maybe you should just accept this condition and learn to live with it". That will get into your heart if you don't put a guard around it. We put a guard dog in our yard to protect our home. Why not put a guard around our heart.

The word "diligence" is the Hebrew word "mishmar" meaning a guard (the man, the post, or the prison); This is a military term, "to man the post". Keep watch over your heart. We are to guard, protect, maintain, and keep a watch over our heart.

How do we do that? By what we watch and hear. Remember, our eyes and ears are the gateway into our heart, so we need to be careful what we watch in the movies on TV.

I am amazed at what some Christians watch. The more junk we watch, the more our heart becomes desensitized to the sin and corruption in this world. If we are not careful we will end up having a reprobate mind and a sick body. So let's guard our heart, for out of it springs the issues of life.

Seventh, for out of it (your heart) spring the issues of life.

The anointing of God's Word and life in your heart will bring forth the issues of healing up out of your spirit man, touching and changing your mortal body.

As you attend to the Word, incline your ear to the Word, not letting them depart from your eyes, keeping them in the midst of your heart. It will bring forth faith and faith in the Word of God is the answer to all your needs.

Zoe, God's life springing up out of your heart by walking in faith, trusting and believing in the healing power of God, will remove all symptoms of sickness and disease in your body. Romans 10:8, But what does it say? "The word is near you, in your mouth and in your heart" (that is, the word of faith which we preach).

2 Corinthians 4:13 "And since we have the same spirit of faith, according to what is written, "I believed and therefore I spoke," we also believe and therefore speak."

We speak what we believe and that is why it is important to keep the Word of God in front of our eyes and in our heart. We need to speak to the symptoms in our body, the pain, sickness and disease. Don't ask God to do anything about the problem; you speak to it in Jesus name. Arthritis, I command you to leave in Jesus name. Pain, I command you to leave in Jesus name. You can not live in my body. My body has been bought by the blood of the lamb.

Jesus said for us to speak to the mountain and that the mountain has to be removed and cast into the sea. This is how faith and healing works. We believe and therefore we speak.

Give your attention to God's Word first and foremost, not to the sickness and disease. Having done all to stand, stand. Stand on the Word of God until you see the manifestation of your healing take place. This is faith in action; it is being a doer of the Word of God. We need to be steadfast and immovable in our faith in the Word of God in the area of healing as well as other areas in our life. Faith activates the healing, anointing power of God to rid you of all diseases.

CHAPTER TWENTY

Making the Impossible, Possible

Jesus is still in the saving, healing, and baptizing in the Holy Spirit business. Nothing is too hard or impossible for Jesus to do. Nothing is impossible.

Because of our limitations as mortal people, we sometimes think that there are situations that we come up against that are impossible, but with God, nothing is impossible. All things are possible with God. If you believe this, then the impossible can take place for you.

> **Mark 9:22-23**
> **22** And often he has thrown him both into the fire and into the water to destroy him. **But if You can do anything,** "have compassion on us and help us." **23** Jesus said to him, **"If you can believe, all things are possible to him who believes."**

The biggest mistake people make is that they are always asking God, "if", if you can heal me, if you will heal me.

"If" is the enemy of faith. It will rob you of your blessings of receiving your healing. Notice what Jesus said; He turned the table around and said "if you can believe, all things are possible to him who believes". Again He put the responsibility on us, not God. If you can believe. "If you can believe all things are possible to him who believes." How many things are possible? "All", that includes your healing.

Life is the same no matter where we live and what time period it is. People who lived during what we call the Old Testament days were no different than those during Jesus' days. Those during Jesus' days are no different than today. The faces are different and the names are different, but we all get attacked from the devil the same way. The answer to our problems is what do we believe to be possible.

Isaiah 38:1-3
1 In those days Hezekiah was sick and near death. And Isaiah the prophet, the son of Amoz, went to him and said to him, "Thus says the LORD: Set your house in order, for you shall die and not live." **2** Then **Hezekiah turned his face toward the wall**, and prayed to the LORD, **3** and said, "Remember now, O LORD, I pray, how I have walked before You in truth and with a loyal heart, and have done what is good in Your sight." And Hezekiah wept bitterly.

How would you like someone to come to you and tell you that you're going to die? That is not a pleasant word. He was sick, so sick he was dying. Not only was he sick and near death, God tells Hezekiah he was going to die.

Hezekiah turned his face to the wall and prayed. That is a good thing to do when we are facing an impossible situation in our life. Why did he turn his face to the wall? Is there any meaning to this? Yes, it means that he turned his face from all opposition. He turned from the prophet Isaiah. He turned from his aching body. He turned from his symptoms. He turned from all those who were telling him to give up and die. He turned from all their doubt and unbelief. He turned from the doctors and turned his face to the wall to where the only thing he could see was GOD. He set his face like flint and looked to God for His great mercy and started to reason with God. Isaiah 1:18 "Come now, and let us reason together," Says the LORD. Hezekiah was reasoning with God, telling Him how he prayed, walked in truth with a loyal heart and did what is good in His sight. He also wept. Now we know that crying and pity does not do us any good, but turning our face toward Him and walking in the truth of the Word of God will deliver us and set us free.

Isaiah 38:4-5
4 And the word of the LORD came to Isaiah, saying, **5** Go and say to Hezekiah, "Thus says the LORD, the God of David your father": "I have heard your prayer, I have seen your tears; surely I will add to your days fifteen years".

Notice Hezekiah did not die, and he did not set his house in order nor did he listen to the prophet Isaiah, but turned his face to the wall, and look what happened. God heard his prayer, saw his tears and gave him fifteen more years to live.

God made the impossible, possible. He turned the tables around. When we keep our face to the wall, so to speak, we are turning our back from all doubt and unbelief, from our pain and looking unto Jesus, the healer of our bodies. Then He would turn the impossible to the possible because "with God, all things are possible".

It takes two to tangle. God could not do His part without

Hezekiah taking responsibility for his own actions. God told the prophet Isaiah to tell King Hezekiah to put his house in order because he was going to die. Some people will say, "see, God does change His mind." No, He doesn't. He did not want the King to die, but He could not bless him if he had not turned his face to the wall and sought God with all of his heart.

If you will notice, even the prophet could not help the King. Too many people are looking for a preacher to help them. They go to some meetings looking for a word from heaven.

If we would just turn our face to the wall and seek God. Too many people are seeking the healing instead of the healer. Christ is our Healer; we need to seek Him.

God is the same yesterday, today, and forever and what He did for the King He will do for you. What worked for him will work for you.

Throughout history there are those who have done great things for God. The only reason they got results was because they turned their faces to the wall (they turned from natural thinking and began to believe God).

Remember the story of Noah. God told him to build an ark to save him and his family. People thought he was crazy, but he did what God told him to do. That was his way of turning his face toward the wall. If we would turn our face to the wall, so to speak, and trust God, He will make the impossible possible.

Another Old Testament account is when Moses was being used by God to bring the children of Israel out of bondage. When Moses went up to seek God, and God appeared in a burning bush and gave him the Ten Commandments, the children of Israel got tired of waiting for him, so they built a golden calf to worship. God would have destroyed the nation if Moses had not stood in the gap and turned his face to the wall (toward God). Moses was looking to God and not the circumstances. He was angry to say the least, but he turned his face to seek after God. God turned the impossible into the possible.

Let's jump over into the New Testament to the Book of Matthew 6:33 "But seek first the kingdom of God and His righteousness, and all these things shall be added to you". All means all. That includes healing from any type of sickness or disease and pain. "Seek first", in essence, is turning your back to the wall and looking to Him, the creator of heaven and earth; the healer of our bodies. "Seek and you will find."

CHAPTER TWENTY ONE

God's Redemptive Names

On pages six and seven of the Scofield Bible, Dr. Scofield, in his footnote on the redemptive names, says that the name "Jehovah" is distinctly the redemptive name of Deity and means "the Self existent One Who reveals Himself". Then he says that these names "point to God's continuous and increasing self revelation".

Jehovah is the personal Name of God in His relationship as Redeemer.

Exodus 3:13-15

13 Then Moses said to God, "Indeed, when I come to the children of Israel and say to them, 'The God of your fathers has sent me to you,' and they say to me, 'What is His name?' what shall I say to them?" **14** And God said to Moses, "I AM WHO I AM." And He said, "Thus you shall say to the children of Israel, I AM has sent me to you". **15** Moreover God said to Moses, "Thus you shall say to the children of Israel: The LORD (**Jehovah**) God of your fathers, the God of Abraham, the God of Isaac, and the God of Jacob, has sent me to you. This is My name forever, and this is My memorial to all generations."

The name Jehovah is also found in Exodus 6:2-3 "And God spoke to Moses and said to him: "I am the LORD (Jehovah)" , I appeared to Abraham, to Isaac, and to Jacob, as God Almighty, but by My name, LORD, (Jehovah) I was not known to them."
Jehovah is the name for the Lord God and His compound names are:

1. Jehovah Elohim.
Genesis 2:4 "This is the history of the heavens and the earth when they were created, in the day that the LORD God (Jehovah Elohim) made the earth and the heavens." This shows the trinity at work creating the generations and the earth.

2. Jehovah Jireh.
Genesis 22:14 "And Abraham called the name of the place, The-Lord-Will-Provide; (Jehovah Jireh) as it is said to this day", "In the Mount of The LORD it shall be provided." God provided an offering for Abraham. He also provided one for us. Romans 8:32 "He who did not spare His own Son, but delivered Him up for us all."

3. Jehovah Nissi.
Exodus 17:15 "And Moses built an altar and called its name, **The-Lord-Is-My-Banner**;" The Israelites just won the battle with Amalek. Aaron and Hur were holding up the hands of Moses during the battle. As long as they were holding up his arms they would win. Because of this they called it the Lord is our banner or victor.

1 Corinthians 15:57 "But thanks be to God, **who gives us the victory through our Lord Jesus Christ.**"

4. Jehovah Shamma.

Ezekiel 48:35 "All the way around shall be eighteen thousand cubits; and the name of the city from that day shall be: **The LORD Is There.**"

Matthew 28:20 "**I am with you always**, even to the end of the age." Amen.

5. Jehovah Tsidkenu.

Jeremiah 23:6 "In His days Judah will be saved, And Israel will dwell safely; Now this is His name by which He will be called: THE LORD OUR RIGHTEOUSNESS." Jesus took our sin and gave us the Righteousness of God. 2 Corinthians 5:21 "For He made Him who knew no sin to be sin for us, **that we might become the righteousness of God in Him.**"

6. Jehovah Ra-ah.

Psalms 23:1 "The LORD is my shepherd." Jesus gave His life for us, we are His sheep. John 10:11 **"I am the good shepherd"**. The good shepherd gives His life for the sheep.

7. Jehovah-Shalom.

Judges 6:24 "So Gideon built an altar there to the LORD, and called it **The-LORD-Is-Peace**. To this day it is still in Ophrah of the Abiezrites." Jesus said He is our peace. John 14:27 "Peace I leave with you, **My peace I give to you**; not as the world gives do I give to you. Let not your heart be troubled, neither let it be afraid."

8. Jehovah Sabaoth.

Psalms 24:10 "Who is this **King of Glory**? The LORD of hosts, He is the King of Glory." No matter how you see it,

Jesus is **OUR** King of Glory. Revelations 19:16 "And He has on His robe and on His thigh a name written: **KING OF KINGS AND LORD OF LORDS.**" He is Jehovah-Sabaoth.

9. Jehovah-Rapha.

> Exodus 15:26 and said, "If you diligently heed the voice of the LORD your God and do what is right in His sight, give ear to His commandments and keep all His statutes, I will put none of the diseases on you which I have brought on the Egyptians. **For I am the LORD who heals you.**"

Exodus 15:26 "for I, the LORD, am your healer."(NASU) "for I am Jehovah that healeth thee." (ASV)

I have left this one for last because I will go into greater detail with Jehovah Rapha than all the others. This is the first covenant promise, statute and ordinance that God gave after the parting of the Red Sea. Exodus 15:26, "For I am the LORD who heals you." (Jehovah-Rapha)

In the New Testament, there is an ordinance that connects with this one and we call it the Lord's Supper. 1 Corinthians 11:26 "For as often as you eat this bread and drink this cup, you proclaim the Lord's death till He comes."

There is healing in the taking of the Lord's Supper because we are proclaiming what He did for us on the cross of Calvary-shedding His blood and taking stripes on His back.

In John 3:16 it says that "God so LOVED the world that He gave His only begotten Son." God the Father sent Jesus to be your Healer. God loves us so much that He was willing to let Jesus take our place. He has vowed in both the Old Testament and the New Testament to save us and heal us.

The word "heal" in the Old Testament is the Hebrew verb (Rapha) which means to repair, restore health, heal, mend, fix and cure.

Genesis 20:17 "So Abraham prayed to God; and God healed Abimelech, his wife, and his female servants. Then they bore children."

Psalms 103:3 "Who forgives all your iniquities, Who heals (Rapha) all your diseases."

Psalms.107:20 "He sent His **Word** and healed (Rapha) them." I especially like this one. John 1:1 "In the beginning was the Word, and the Word was with God, and the Word was God." In the beginning was the Word. That is talking about Jesus. Jesus and the Holy written Word, the Bible, are the same.

The participle form of Rapha is "rophe," which means doctor, physician. 2 Chronicles 16:12 "And in the thirty-ninth year of his reign, Asa became diseased in his feet, and his malady was severe; yet in his disease he did not seek the LORD, but the physicians." (Rophe)Exodus 15:26 "I am the LORD who heals you." "I am Jehovah, your rophe", your Doctor, Physician and healer.

Now let's jump over to the New Testament. We are going to look at Greek words translated from Heal and Healing in verbs and nouns.

(Verbs) Matthew 14:36 "And besought him that they might only touch the hem of his garment: and as many as touched were made perfectly whole." (KJV)

diosozo NT:1295, "to save thoroughly" (dia), is used in the passive voice and rendered "**were made whole**" (from Vine's Expository Dictionary of Biblical Words).

Acts 14:9 "he had faith to be **healed**", (sozo). (NKJV) HEAL, HEALING

 sozo NT:4982, "to save," is translated by the verb "to heal" in the KJV of Mark 5:23 and Luke 8:36 (RV, "**to make whole**"; so KJV frequently); the idea is that of saving from disease and it's effects. (from Vine's Expository Dictionary of Biblical Words).

Matthew 4:23 "And Jesus went about all Galilee, teaching in their synagogues, preaching the gospel of the kingdom, and **healing** (Therapeuo) all kinds of sickness and all kinds of disease among the people."

Therapeuo NT: 2323 primarily signifies "to serve as a therapon, an attendant"; then, **"to care for the sick, to treat, cure, heal"** (from Vine's Expository Dictionary of Biblical Words).

(Nouns) Luke 9:11 "He received them and spoke to them about the kingdom of God, and healed those who had need of healing." (Therapeia), therapeia NT:2322, akin to A, No. 1, primarily denotes **"care, attention,"** Luke 12:42 (see HOUSEHOLD); then, **"medical service, healing"** (from Vine's Expository Dictionary of Biblical Words).

Health - Acts 27:34 "Wherefore I pray you to take some meat: for this is for your health"(KJV)

Note: In Acts 27:34, **soteria, "salvation, safety,"** is translated "health" in the KJV; the RV, gives the right meaning, **"safety."** (from Vine's Expository Dictionary of Biblical Words).

The word health is translated "Therapeuo" in Strongs Concordance # 2323 which is where we get our English word therapy and therapeutic. Jesus gave His disciples and you and me authority to use His name to heal (therapeuo) all those who believe in the healing power of God.

Luke 10:9 "And heal (therapeuo) the sick there, and say to them, 'The kingdom of God has come near to you.'"

Luke 10:19 "Behold, I give you the authority to trample on serpents and scorpions, and over all the power of the enemy, and nothing shall by any means hurt you." We are to treat, cure, and administer the healing power of God into the lives of other people.

CHAPTER TWENTY TWO

The Omnipotent Power of God

The word omnipotent is a theological term that refers to the all encompassing power of God. Omnipotence means "the quality or state of being omnipotent. An agency or force of unlimited power" (Webster's Ninth New Collegiate Dictionary).

Throughout the Bible from Genesis to Revelation, we see the power of the Lord God Almighty. We see His unlimited power in the creation of the earth and mankind.

Genesis 1:1 "In the beginning God created the heavens and the earth". How much power do you think it took to create the heavens and the earth? Can you do that? I know I do not have the power to do that.

There is a total of fourteen times in Genesis that God either said "God called or God said". He had the power to create the stars, the sun, and the moon, all the fish of the sea, and the foul of the air. God created the earth and the fullness of it. When He was all done, He spoke to His Son, Jesus, and the Holy Spirit and said "let us make man in our own image, according to Our likeness". Genesis 1:26.

Jeremiah 32:16-17 "Ah, Lord GOD! Behold, You have made the heavens and the earth by **Your great power** and outstretched arm. **There is nothing too hard for You**."

Throughout history, people have tried to find a contradiction in God's Omnipotent Power by saying "God cannot do everything. He cannot lie, cheat, steal, sin, or go against His Holy Written Word". All that is true. He will not go against His Word. In no way does this do away with His almighty power. It shows His self-limitation of His will. He will not go against His nature or His Word.

Psalms139:14 "I will praise You, for I am fearfully and wonderfully made; Marvelous are Your works, And that my soul knows very well."

Ephesians 2:10 "For we are His workmanship"

When God created man, He made us in His image. We are a piece of art, His handy-work. In His work there are no flaws, no sickness or disease or pain. Do you think for a minute that God cannot touch your body and make it whole, like it was created to be? There is no sickness in heaven and therefore cannot be in the Father, Son, or the Holy Ghost. And sickness cannot stay in His handy-work.

If God can create the earth as we know it, and part the Red Sea, turn water into blood, turn water into wine, and then we have the nerve to say that He cannot heal us! That is one of the most blasphemous things I have ever heard.

We all know the story of the three Hebrew boys who were thrown into a fiery furnace. They had faith in their God that He would deliver them.

Daniel 3:17 "If that is the case, our God whom we serve is able to deliver us from the burning fiery furnace.

They knew the power of their God. Our God is the same as their God and He has the same power to work in our behalf.

God the Father raised Jesus from the dead. Jesus raised Lazarus from the dead. This shows the power of God over death. Jesus by His word calmed the sea, Matthew 8:26 "But He said to them, "Why are you fearful, O you of little faith?" Then He arose and rebuked the winds and the sea, and there was a great calm." I call that Power from the Almighty God. We need to see and know the power of God for what it really is. If God can do all this, then He can touch and heal your body. Genesis 18:14 "Is anything too hard for the LORD?" I think not.

At this point someone is probably thinking what about the Sovereignty of God? Good question, I am glad you asked.

Ephesians 1:4-5

4 Just as He chose us in Him before the foundation of the world, that we should be holy and without blame before Him in love, **5** having **predestined** us to adoption as sons by Jesus Christ to Himself, according to the good pleasure of **His will**.

A lot of people will use this verse of scripture to argue that God has predestined some to be sick in their body, or even go so far as to say He has predestined some to be saved and some not to be saved. Let's look at its counterpart. John says in Revelation 22:17 (B) "he that **will** let him take the water of life freely." (The Worrell New Testament).

John 5:40 "But you are not **willing** to come to Me that you may have life."

John 10:10 "The thief does not come except to steal, and to kill, and to destroy. I have come that they may have life, and that they may have it more abundantly."

It is evident and true that the Bible teaches both views. God is Sovereign, but not arbitrary. We have a free will; we can make our own choices in life. God wants to see us whole, healed and well. And to be real honest with you, that is how He sees you and me. He sees us through the Blood of

His Son. He sees us healed. We need to believe in His omnipotent power to touch and heal every part of our body from the top of our head to the tip of our toes. He can only do what we allow Him to do on our behalf. He is sitting up in heaven full of grace and power to be poured out upon you for your healing.

Make your mind up that you will be as bold as the Roman Soldier who came to Jesus and said "Just speak the Word and my son will be made whole". Be like the woman with the issue of blood who said "if I may only touch the hem of His garment I shall be whole". The Bible says you can have what you say. So lay hold of the Word of God for your healing and let His power touch you.

CHAPTER TWENTY THREE

Take Back What the Devil Stole

Have you ever had anything stolen from you? Well, I have. The first time was when I was about thirteen years old. I had a weight bench for lifting weights and a guy I knew wanted to borrow it. I really did not want him to borrow it, but I let him. When I asked for it back, he would not give it back to me. So my dad went to his home and got it back for me. The second time is when someone wanted to borrow my motorcycle. It was a 250 Yamaha Special. Again, I let some guy use it and when I asked for it back, he would not give it to me. I had to make an issue of the matter and stand my ground. In the same manner, that is the devil's job, to steal from us our health and healing. What we do about it is up to us.

John 10:10 "The thief (the devil) does not come except to **steal, and to kill, and to destroy.** I have come that they may have life, and that they may have it more abundantly." Rest assured we are in a battle to the end and the devil will not give up.

NT: 2813 a. to steal; absolutely, to commit a theft: b.

153

transitive, to steal i. e. take away by stealth: tina, the dead body of one, (from Thayer's Greek Lexicon).

To kill is to sacrifice, immolate, to slay, kill, and to slaughter. Thayer's Greek Lexicon.

Destroy, NT:622, to destroy i. e. to put out of the way entirely, abolish, put an end to, ruin: metaphorically, to devote or give over to eternal misery: (from Thayer's Greek Lexicon).

Let's look again at the fact that the devil wants to steal. He wants to steal your family, finances, home, and your health. It is up to us to use our God-given authority to take back what the devil has stolen, to take back our health and healing.

Authority is the circuit or channel in which the power operates. We cannot have authority without power. You cannot have power without authority.

I like to use the illustration of a policeman. During a traffic accident there are policemen that are directing traffic. An officer does not have the physical strength and power to stop a Semi-truck, but his badge and a gun on his hip gives him the authority to stop traffic.

Matthew 28:18 "And Jesus came and spoke to them, saying, "All authority has been given to Me in heaven and on earth." God did not lose His power when Adam fell. God lost His circuit or channel of authority from which to release His power.

When God sent Jesus down from heaven, He did not come to get back God's power, but to restore divine authority to man through His death, burial, and resurrection. So in this verse of scripture, Jesus was telling His disciples that all the authority God gave Him, He was giving to them, and that applies to us as well.

When we use the name of Jesus, all hell comes to attention.

Philippians 2:10 "That at the name of Jesus every knee should bow, of those in heaven, and of those on earth, and of those under the earth." Jesus said that we could use His name to combat the enemy. In other words, we have all heaven backing us up as we use His name. Just like the policeman has all of the city backing him up when he is directing traffic.

When Jesus was led up into heaven to be with the Father, Satan did not lose his authority on this earth, but it gave Jesus more power and authority over the devil. And He gave us His name and authority to use against sickness and disease.

> **Ephesians 1:18-23**
> **18** the eyes of your understanding being enlighten; that you may know what is the hope of his calling, what are the riches of the glory of His inheritance in the saints, **19** and what is the exceeding greatness of His power toward us who believe, according to the working of His mighty power **20** which He worked in Christ when He raised Him from the dead and seated Him at His right hand in the heavenly places, **21** far above all principality and power (authorities) and might and dominion, and every name that is named, not only in this age (the church age) but also in that which is to come. **22** And He put **all things (sickness and disease) under His feet,** and gave **Him** to be head over all things to the church, **23** which is His body, the fullness of Him who fills all in all.

All things means all things, including sickness and disease.

Jesus is the head of the body, the church. We are the church, you and me. God placed us just under Jesus and gave us His authority. When the church wakes up to this truth, then they will stop asking God or Jesus to do something about the devil and realize we have authority, dominion, and power over him.

You may be thinking, "well I don't know about all this; all this seems so far fetched. You are making us out to be God." No, we are not God, but He gave us His power. Luke 10:17 "Then the seventy returned with joy, saying, "Lord, even the **demons are subject to us in Your name**." **All** sickness and disease comes from the devil or demons. The demons were subject to the name of Jesus, not the seventy.

I can not emphasize it enough! The devil and demons must obey us when we use the name of Jesus, but we need to be submitted to God. We can take back our health. The devil stole our health and healing and it is up to us to bind and rebuke the enemy and take back what the devil stole from us.

We all know the story of the seven sons of Sceva, how some Jewish exorcists tried to cast the demons out of them and they could not. Acts 19:15 "And the evil spirit answered and said, "Jesus I know, and Paul I know; but who are you?"

The devil and demons are not subject to Tom, Bill, Sue, Mary, or any other person for that matter. They are only subject to the name of Jesus. Every knee shall bow at that name in heaven and on earth.

James 4:7 "Therefore submit to God. Resist the devil and he will flee from you". Most people are trying to resist the devil; they are trying to bind and rebuke the enemy and take back their healing without submitting to God. You will not be able to see the devil and demons with their sickness and disease flee unless you are submitted to God. To have authority you must be under authority. The policeman has authority to stop traffic on the highway because he is under authority. Authority and faith, and knowing who you are in Christ, go hand in hand. If you are truly submitted to God, you will be going to church, paying your tithes, and serving the Lord in any area in your local church.

Notice it said "Jesus I know, and Paul I know, but who

are you?" Jesus was submitted to God, the Father. Paul was submitted to Jesus. When we are submitted to God, the devil must, I said must obey, as we use the name of Jesus. It has to be mixed with faith and knowing who we are in Christ.

We had a substance abuse group in our church at one time. The person who was heading it up came to me one time and said that there was this lady who was in bad shape. It was beyond what he was ready to deal with and he asked me if I would see her, so I said yes. She came to our church on a Wednesday night, but sat in her car till service was over. When most of the people were gone, I went out to see her. Her car was running and the stereo was playing, so I asked her to turn off the stereo and she asked me why. I told her so I could talk to her better. She turned it off. Then I asked her to turn off the engine of her car and she did. I had my hands resting on the door where the window was and one of the men who was there with me told me she had a razor blade in her hand. I quickly moved my arms and hands away from the car. Her eyes never left me, everywhere I walked, her eyes followed me. I started commanding the demons to come out of her. I had made my way around to the other side of the car and when I commanded the demons to come out, she quickly jumped out of the car, ran to the other side where I was and made a fist at me. I had a couple of guys hold her arms. We tried to get her into the church, but she would not just walk in on her own. Someone said that she or the demons would follow me right on in, so as I was walking backwards to the church she followed me right on in. From that time on, we spent about three hours commanding the demons to come out of her. When we were done she asked for her crutches, she was unable to walk without her crutches. Get this picture in your mind. I used my faith, my authority, and the name of Jesus to command the demons to come out of her. Before we left we had her receive the Lord. The next day she called and thanked my wife for what we did.

If I had not been submitted to God, known who I am in Christ, and used my authority, that would not have ended that way. Mark 16:17 "And these signs will follow those who believe: In My name they will cast out demons;"

Matthew 28:18-20
18 And Jesus came and spoke to them, saying, "All authority has been given to Me in heaven and on earth. **19** Go therefore and make disciples of all the nations, baptizing them in the name of the Father and of the Son and of the Holy Spirit, **20** teaching them to observe all things that I have commanded you; and lo, I am with you always, even to the end of the age." Amen.

Philippians 2:10 "That at the name of Jesus every knee should bow, of those in heaven, and of those on earth, and of those under the earth."

Luke 10:19 "Behold, I give you the authority to trample on serpents and scorpions, and over all the power of the enemy."

Romans 5:17 "For if by the one man's offense death reigned through the one, much more those who receive abundance of grace and of the gift of righteousness will **reign in life through the One, Jesus Christ.**"

To reign you have to have authority. Again, Jesus gave His disciples authority and we are His disciples. We reign through Jesus using His name and speaking or pleading His blood, taking our authority in Him.

Take back your health and healing by using your God-given authority. The devil and demons have to obey you when you use the name of Jesus.

CHAPTER TWENTY FOUR

The Praise Cure

On one of Len Menk's music CD, it makes mention of a phrase of the old-time Pentecostals. They would say, "let's have a praise cure". They were talking about praise and worshipping their way to healing. Praise and Worship will bring victory and healing to you. It is one of the ways that will get God to bring forth His healing anointing to touch and administer healing to your body.

The greatest cure known to mankind can be found in praising God. The greatest deliverance known to man is within the reach of every believer on this earth and it is found in praising God from a sincere heart of love and gratitude! (Kenneth Hagin Jr., The Untapped Power in Praise).

In her book, Healing from Heaven, Dr. Lilian B. Yeomans tells the story about a woman who went to China as a missionary many years ago when China was open to receiving the gospel. This missionary contracted smallpox. In those days no cure existed for this disease, so doctors could do little for her. If a person contracted smallpox back then, there was no hope-the person just died. It was a deadly disease. This missionary was quarantined in her room, and ugly smallpox marks covered her body from the top of her head to the soles of her feet. There she was, stricken with a deadly disease with little medical assistance, destitute, and in a faraway country, virtually given up to die. She didn't know what to do since there was no cure, so she began fervently to seek the Lord. God spoke to her and told her to praise Him for His faithfulness, to keep His own Word.

She sang praises to God from her heart; she did nothing but praise the Lord. She praised Him for His greatness. She praised Him for all that He had ever done for her. She praised Him for His faithfulness to His Word. She praised Him for her healing. She praised God, and praised God, and praised God.

After several days of heartfelt praise, the Lord showed her that the praise- basket was full! She walked out of that quarantined room completely healed! Her skin was as smooth and clear as a child's; no smallpox marks were to be found anywhere on her body. (Kenneth Hagin Jr. the Untapped Power in Praise).

Mark 11:24 says to believe that you received the answer to your prayers when you pray. If you believe that you have received them, then the next thing to do is to have a praise cure. In other words, keep praising Him for His Word. Keep praising Him that you have what you prayed for and the answer to your prayers. Because He is faithful to watch over His Word in our lives.

1 Corinthians 10:11 says that the Old Testament was written for our example. We can learn and grow from what they have gone through and have done. Here is the account of Ammon, Moab and Mont Seir being defeated because Jahaziel listened to God and trusted and obeyed Him and His Word.

2 Chronicles 20:14-22
14 Then the Spirit of the LORD came upon

Jahaziel the son of Zechariah, the son of Benaiah, the son of Jeiel, the son of Mattaniah, a Levite of the sons of Asaph, in the midst of the assembly. **15** And he said, "Listen, all you of Judah and you inhabitants of Jerusalem, and you, King Jehoshaphat! Thus says the LORD to you: Do not be afraid nor dismayed because of this great multitude, for the battle is not yours, but God's. **16** Tomorrow go down against them. They will surely come up by the Ascent of Ziz, and you will find them at the end of the brook before the Wilderness of Jeruel. **17** You will not need to fight in this battle. Position yourselves, stand still and see the salvation of the LORD, who is with you, O Judah and Jerusalem!' Do not fear or be dismayed; tomorrow go out against them, for the LORD is with you." **18** And Jehoshaphat bowed his head with his face to the ground, and all Judah and the inhabitants of Jerusalem bowed before the LORD, worshiping the LORD. **19** Then the Levites of the children of the Kohathites and of the children of the Korahites stood up to praise the LORD God of Israel with voices loud and high. **20** So they rose early in the morning and went out into the Wilderness of Tekoa; and as they went out, Jehoshaphat stood and said, "Hear me, O Judah and you inhabitants of Jerusalem: Believe in the LORD your God, and you shall be established; believe His prophets, and you shall prosper." **21** And when he had consulted with the people, he appointed those who should sing to the LORD, and who should praise the beauty of holiness, as they went out before the army and were saying: "Praise the LORD, For His mercy endures forever." **22** Now when they began to sing and to praise, the LORD set ambushes against the people of Ammon, Moab, and Mount Seir, who had come against Judah; and they were defeated.

Notice verse fifteen says the battle is not yours, but God's. The battle of winning over sickness and disease is not your battle, but God's. He won the battle when Jesus nailed our sickness to the cross. Give Him praise for that.

In verse seventeen, it says to position yourself and stand. Their position was one of praise and thanksgiving because the battle was already won by God. When you know you have won the battle before you see the results, don't you start praising God? Or do you sit there thinking how are we going to win this one. Look at what they did in verse eighteen. They bowed their heads and worshipped the Lord. Why?

Because God had already told them the battle was not theirs, but God's. They knew that they had won before they fought the battle. In verse nineteen, it says that they praised God with voices loud and high. Why? Because they knew they won before it was over.

Verse twenty says to believe in the Lord and you will be established. Have you ever noticed when a parent makes a promise to a child, that child believes what the parent says, such as "I will take you to Disney World for your birthday", the child starts to jump up and down, praising and thanking his parents before they even get there. This holds true for us when God says do not be afraid, the battle is not yours, but mine. We should enter into praise and thanksgiving for the answer to our healing.

Verses twenty-one and twenty-two show how they went out singing "Praise the Lord, for His mercy endures forever." When they began to sing, the Lord set ambushes against their enemies and they were defeated.

Our enemies are sickness and disease, pain and suffering. They have been defeated by Jesus Christ who took stripes upon His back for our healing. "By His stripes you were healed."

In the world of sports, you have a defensive team and an offensive team. In this account, God told the children of Israel to be on the offensive side. The offensive side is one of praise and thanksgiving. They were not to defend themselves, but trust and believe in the one who went before them and defeated the army for them. They were to praise God because God took care of the battle for them. Just like Jesus took care of our battle of sickness and disease.

Let's look at the New Testament. Hebrews 13:15 "Therefore by Him let us continually offer the **sacrifice** of praise to God, that is, the fruit of our lips, giving thanks to His name". Quite often it is a sacrifice to praise and worship, and give thanks to the Lord when our bodies are screaming with pain and we haven't gotten the sleep we need. What a sacrifice, but we are the ones who will get blessed as we do give Him praise for our healing.

1 Peter 1:7 "That the genuineness of your faith, being much more precious than gold that perishes, though it is tested by fire, may be found to **praise**, honor, and glory at the revelation of Jesus Christ."

Here were two guys whose faith was so genuine that God performed a miracle for them. Even when they were locked up in prison and their feet in stocks, they did not lose their faith in the Lord, but rather gave praise and thanksgiving. Most people would have given up if they went through what these two guys went through. But no, they sang and praised their way to victory.

Acts 16:25-26
25 But at midnight Paul and Silas were praying and singing hymns to God, and the prisoners were listening to them. **26** Suddenly there was a great earthquake, so that the foundations of the prison were shaken; and immediately all the doors were opened and everyone's chains were loosed.

You may be in your midnight hour, so to speak. That happens to be the darkest time in your life. When you are looking at the doctor's report and he is telling you "there is nothing we can do; you have six months to live." Start praising the Lord, "for He is good and His mercy endures forever".

Notice that the prisoners heard them. We are not to be quiet about praising Him. We are to shout it from the rooftops, not just in church, but everywhere we go. Let the Lord know that you love Him and trust Him.

Paul and Silas had a faith that was so genuine, so real, that when the guards told them to shut up, they just praised and worshipped the Lord and all heard them.

You can tell what is in you, faith or doubt, when you are in your midnight hour. "Out of the abundance of the heart the mouth speaks." We need to be built up in the Word of God, so when the enemy attacks us with sickness and disease, we can praise our way out of it.

1 Corinthians 15:57 "But thanks be to God, who gives us the victory through our Lord Jesus Christ." Give Him thanks, praise, and worship because we have the victory.

Psalms 34:1 "I will bless the LORD at all times; His praise shall continually be in my mouth."

Psalms 107:21-22
21 Oh, that men would give thanks to the LORD for His goodness, and for His wonder-

ful works to the children of men! **22** Let them sacrifice the sacrifices of thanksgiving, And declare His works with rejoicing.

You might be thinking, how much and how long should I praise the Lord? Well, how much do you want to be healed? You praise Him till you have the answer. Some people only give the Lord a few minutes in the morning. They're having coffee and eating their toast and taking a scripture promise out of their little box. They look at the scripture and off to work they go. Some give more time to sports, hobbies, work and social life than they do to worshipping the Lord. Some marriages are failing because they don't give time to their family. We need to give plenty of time to the Lord and our family.

Do you remember the story of the walls of Jericho, how they came falling down? God told the Israelites to march around Jericho everyday without making a sound. On the seventh day, God told them to march around Jericho seven times, and as they marched on the seventh day, they were to blow their trumpets and praise God. When they did this, the walls came crashing down. Joshua 6:16,20

Do you want the walls of sickness and disease to come falling down? These people acted in pure unadulterated faith to the man of God (Joshua) leading them into victory. When your pastor tells you how to be free, you need to listen and obey, if it lines up with the Word of God.

Praise and worship touches the heartstrings of God. He inhabits the praises of His people. God is not an egotistical maniac up in heaven saying, "Come on you people. Don't you know I want you to praise me. Praise me, you hear me. I want you to praise me, praise me." No! He knows that praise and worship is another gateway to receiving your healing.

Psalms 9:1 "I will praise You, O LORD, with my whole heart; (I will tell of all Your marvelous works). Praise Him with your whole heart. No matter who is watching or who is not. Give Him your whole heart in Praise and Worship.

There is a song on the market and the words go like this. "I give you praise for you deserve it, I give you praise for what you've done, I give you praise for you are able. I'll give you praise until I overcome. I give you praise when the sun is shining. I give you praise in the dark of night. I give you praise when the battle rages. I give you praise until it works out right." That is what we need to do. Give Him praise until it works out right. Until we are walking in the full manifestation of our healing.

You might be thinking, when do I praise Him? Depending on who you listen to as to when you should spend time praising the Lord, you can become really confused as to a certain time. Some will take you to Psalms 63:1 where King David says he will rise early to seek the Lord. That was good back then, but what if you have a night job? You can't rise early, you're already up. Some people are early risers and others do better late at night. Don't get into bondage as to the time-just do it! Some people try to set a certain time and place to worship the Lord. That is fine as long as your schedule does not get messed up. I know some people who are too rigid. They need to be more flexible. If you want to set a time and place to praise God, if five in the morning in your den is fine, then great! If two in the morning in your spare room is a good time, then fine. Don't just worship Him for five minutes, worship Him for one, two, or three hours. God has no watch. He is not a clock watcher like some people are. They are watching the clock the whole time the preacher is preaching. Some people will say I am going to pray for an hour. What if God moves and wants you to go on longer. He has no watch or clock.

Praise Him because He deserves it; praise Him because He is God, the creator of the heavens and the earth, as well as creating you in the likeness of His own image.

Another song goes like this. "Praise Him, Praise Him, Praise Him in the morning, Praise Him in the noontime, Praise Him, Praise Him, Praise Him when the sun goes down. Let's be true Praisers of God.

CHAPTER TWENTY FIVE

Put Me in Remembrance

We have a tendency to doubt people in life, and rightfully so because of being let down so many times. As a result of this, we usually remind people of a promise they told us. Were you serious when you said you would give me your car, you know you said you would. This is in the negative sense.

God has given us a book of promises and He has never let us down. He said what He meant, and He meant what He said. When He said in Isaiah "by His stripes you are healed", and in 1 Peter 2:24 "by His stripes you were healed". He meant it. Isaiah 43:26 "Put Me in remembrance; Let us contend together; State your case, that you may be acquitted."

While we are standing on the Word, God said to remind Him of His Word. He knows what we need and what we are believing God for, but He wants us to put Him in remembrance of His own Word. (Put me in remembrance) is the Hebrew word "zakar" and means to mention, be mindful, recount, and to make mention of. We are to make mention of His word to Him.

Because of the persistent widow woman, the unjust judge gave her what she needed.

> **Luke 18:1-8**
> **1** Then He spoke a parable to them, that men always ought to pray and not lose heart, **2** saying: "There was in a certain city a judge who did not fear God nor regard man. **3** Now there was a widow in that city; and she came to him, saying, Get justice for me from my adversary. **4** And he would not for a while; but afterward he said within himself, Though I do not fear God nor regard man, **5** yet because this widow troubles me I will avenge her, lest by her continual coming she weary me." **6** Then the Lord said, "Hear what the unjust judge said. **7** And shall God not avenge His own elect who cry out day and night to Him, though He bears long with them? **8** I tell you that He will avenge them speedily. Nevertheless, when the Son of Man comes, will He really find faith on the earth?"

Just as this woman was persistent in presenting her case to the judge, we need to put God in remembrance of His Word. We do this by speaking His Word to Him. Say, "Father you said by the stripes of Jesus I was healed, therefore I am healed. It is your Word and you are faithful to perform it in my life. Thank you so much Lord, I receive it by faith." We don't beg, plead, and cry. We remind Him by thanking Him.

> Back to Isaiah 43:26, It also said to "let us contend together" (It says plead in the KJV) The word plead in Hebrew is shaphat

OT:8199 pronounce sentence (for or against); by implication, to vindicate or punish; by extenssion, to govern; passively, to litigate (literally or figuratively):

We are to pronounce a sentence against Satan, against his sickness and disease and send it back to the pit of hell and claim, receive and walk in our healing, that we may be acquitted. (It says "justified" in the KJV)

Justified is the Hebrew word "tsadaq," to make right in a moral or forensic sense Strongs Concordance # 6663

In context, it is talking about sin, but we can use this verse in any area of our life where we are standing on His Word and claiming His promises in our life. He wants us healed more than we want it.

Let's jump back a few chapters and look at the twin scripture of Isaiah 43 and look in chapter one. Isaiah 1:18 "Come now, and let us reason together," Says the LORD. We are to reason with Him concerning His Word and our healing.

Have you ever been involved in a car accident where you were both right and both wrong and you had to come to some kind of understanding or agreement. Maybe you did not want the police involved with a report so the two of you had to talk things out-reason together. Let's say one turned in front of the other, but the other one was going way beyond the speed limit to stop quickly enough before hitting the one who turned in front of you. So you both get out of the cars and look at the damage and one says there is a parts manager at an auto store and he can get the parts for cost. The other guy says he owns an auto paint shop. So they reason together and help each other out. That is what we are to do with the Word of God, and God Himself.

Talk to God. He will listen to you and your reasonings. "You know, God, that I really don't have much money, and even if I did, the doctors don't need it. I would rather give it to you. (You have to be a person of your word) and besides that your Word says that Jesus took all of my sickness, disease and pain so I would not have to bear it. I want to enjoy life the way life is meant to be enjoyed. You sent your Son to shed His blood and take stripes upon His back for me so that I would receive His healing power in my body." That is how we need to reason with God and you will be surprised. He will agree with you because you are agreeing with His Holy Written Word.

The Hebrew word for reason is "yakach" Strongs Concordance # 3198 and it is a primitive root meaning, to be right (i.e. correct); reciprocal, to argue; causatively, to decide, justify or convict: -appoint, argue, chasten, convince, correct (-ion), daysman, dispute, judge, maintain, plead, reason (together), rebuke, reprove (-r), surely, in any wise.

In Isaiah 53:4 the Hebrew word "griefs" is translated "sickness" everywhere else.

This may sound arrogant, but it's not. I am totally right, no questions asked. Healing belongs to me, it is mine and the devil must take his hands off of me because of what the Word says.

Now some people would say that was being arrogant, but it's not. It is knowing who you are and what legally belongs to you, and you're taking your rightful stand and letting the devil and all the world know that you are healed.

It is not who we are, but whose we are. We are His children. The Bible says that Jesus is the King of kings and the Lord of lords. He is the big King and we are the little king. Kings get to rule and reign in this life. I am going to rule and reign in the area of healing. How about You?

As you begin to reason with the Lord concerning His promises, you will begin to build yourself up in faith to receive your healing.

CHAPTER TWENTY SIX

Why Faith?

Chapter three of this book is talking about your faith making you whole. This chapter will deal with why faith is so important. God's will is for you to be healed and whole.

I have shown you from the beginning of the Bible to the end of it that healing took place in Bible days and that healing is still taking place today. He is the "same yesterday, today and forever".

I've said it before and I will say it again. He wants you healed more than you want to be healed. You will never get anything from God without faith, including your healing.

Hebrews 11:6 "But without faith it is impossible to please Him." It takes faith to believe you can be born again. It takes faith to believe in a heaven to gain and a hell to shun. It takes faith to believe God hears you when you pray. It takes faith to walk in divine health and healing.

Hebrews 10:38 "Now the just shall live by faith; But if anyone draws back, My soul has no pleasure in him." If anyone draws back from living a life of faith, God has no pleasure or joy in them. I know a lot of people who started out in faith, but quit because they did not receive the results quickly enough.

Hosea 4:6 "My people are destroyed for lack of knowledge". If people are not in the healing scriptures and in a church that teaches healing, they will be destroyed because they will always add the faith destroying words, "if it be your will". If implies doubt, and doubt is the enemy of faith. You will not receive your healing by prayers of doubt "if". You will "if" yourself right into the grave, if you are not careful. Faith that takes from God is based on the knowledge of the written Word of God.

3 John 2 "Beloved, I pray that you may prosper in all things and be in health, just as your soul prospers". The word prosper, in the Greek, NT:2137 euodoo (yoo-od-o'-o); from a compound of NT:2095 and NT:3598; to help on the road, i.e. (passively) succeed in reaching; figuratively, to succeed in business affairs:

We are to succeed in reaching our total healing. The words "be in health" mean to have sound health, be well in body. Strongs Concordance # 5198. Even as your soul (your mind, will, emotions, and intellect) prospers.

In other words, if our mind is not prospering, and growing in the things of God in the area of faith and healing then we will not prosper in health.

Faith begins where the will of God is known. So if we are not hearing about faith and healing then we cannot grow in this area.

Romans 10:17 "So then faith comes by hearing, and hearing by the word of God". We need to keep hearing and hearing and hearing the Word on faith and healing for it to produce the end result in our life.

There are many critics out there who will deny the healing power of God, but just because some people say it is not true does not mean it is not so. I like to follow success, and the children of Israel got delivered.

Psalms 105:37 "He also brought them out with silver and gold, and there was none **feeble** among His tribes". No one was sick, lame, blind, or crippled. They all came out healed. It took faith for them to be led out of bondage, (sickness is bondage) and it will take faith for us to get out of the bondage of sickness.

A lot of people think faith and hope are the same, but they are not. The difference is like night and day. Hope is always in the future tense. Well, I hope I get better; I hope I don't lose my job; I hope they don't repossess my car. That is fear and doubt looking to the future.

Faith says I am healed now! Not going to be, but I am healed now!

Hebrews 11:1 says "Now faith is". This is present tense. If someone comes up for prayer and I pray for them and ask them if they're healed, if they say I hope so, they won't get it. If they say, "of course, because the Word says I am and you prayed for me that I am healed". That person will go away healed, whether they feel it or not, because they are in faith.

When you prayed the sinners prayer, did you walk away saved? Of course, because the Bible says we are "saved by Grace through faith". Then it says, if we confess with our mouth and believe in our heart, we will be saved-not going to be-but we are. Faith is not a hoping, wishing, or wanting. It is believing that you have what you prayed for when you prayed. Hope is a good waiter, but a poor receiver." (Dr. Kenneth E. Hagin. New Thresholds of Faith).

Real faith contradicts circumstances. Look into the Biblical history of all the men and women of God who obeyed in the face of their circumstances that were in total contradiction to nature.

Hebrews 11:7 "By faith Noah, being divinely warned of things not yet seen, moved with godly fear."

175

Hebrews 11:8 "By faith Abraham obeyed when he was called to go out to the place which he would receive as an inheritance."

Hebrews 11:11 "By faith Sarah herself also received strength to conceive seed, and she bore a child when she was past the age."

Hebrews 11:17 "By faith Abraham, when he was tested, offered up Isaac."

Hebrews 11:24 "By faith Moses, when he became of age, refused to be called the son of Pharaoh's daughter."

Hebrews 11:27 "By faith he forsook Egypt."

Hebrews 11:29 "By faith they passed through the Red Sea as by dry land."

Hebrews 11:30 "By faith the walls of Jericho fell down after they were encircled for seven days."

Do you see the picture? The best thing of all is that it is a life of faith. It is a lifestyle. Some people say they will try it for a while but they will soon be let down because it is a lifestyle. I preached a message titled the "Lifestyle of the Born-again Christian". The lifestyle of the person of faith will always be rewarded.

Hebrews 11:6 "But without faith it is impossible to please Him, for he who comes to God must believe that He is, and that He is a rewarder of those who diligently seek Him". As you seek Him instead of your healing, He will reward you with healing.

People can be a big hindrance to your faith walk and you need to be a person who won't quit regardless of what others say. It may be your parents, children, doctors, and even your pastor. But don't quit! Your faith will see you through.

Remember the story of blind Bartimaeus in Mark 10:46-52 He heard of Jesus coming his way and he would cry out, "Jesus have mercy on me". And everyone close by told him to be quiet and mind his own business and he cried out even more. "Jesus Son of David have mercy on me." He had a faith in Jesus that would not quit.

I have talked to a lot of people doing different things from owning their own company to some kind of sport or hobby and those who will not give up always get the end result they are after. Why not have the same bull dog tenacity when it comes to the things of God? I will not lose. I will not fail. And I will walk in total manifestation of my healing, because I am working the Word and I will not give up.

Matt 11:12 "And from the days of John the Baptist until now the kingdom of heaven suffers violence, and the violent take it by force."

We need to become forceful and take back our healing. The Bible says,

"Having done all to stand, stand." We are in a spiritual fight. The Word says to fight the good fight of faith. A good fight is one that you win. Become a prizefighter in the Kingdom of God. Lay hold of the Word of God and declare it to be true and working in your life. Philippians 3:13, " but I press on, that I may lay hold of that for which Christ Jesus has also laid hold of me". Paul said he was pressing on that he would lay hold of that which Jesus did for him. Jesus took our sickness and pain. All we need to do is lay hold of it or receive it. Notice what else he did.

Philippians 3:14 "I press toward the goal for the prize of the upward call of God in Christ Jesus". Getting closer to the Lord should be the goal. As we reach that goal we receive the prize of our healing.

Don't quit, because faith in Him will always bring a God-blessing into your life as you so faithfully seek Him.

CHAPTER TWENTY SEVEN

Your Daily Prescription

It doesn't matter what people say about healing. What does the Bible have to say about it? Proverbs 4:20 says to attend to His Word because His Word is health to all our flesh. The Hebrew word for health in verse twenty-two is the word medicine. God's Word is medicine to all our flesh.

Remember God is no respecter of persons. What He has done for one, He will do for you. He "shows no partiality". Acts 10:34 if we take our medicine daily, it will produce healing in us.

The statements you are about to read are taken from the NKJV of the Bible. I will start with the Old Testament:

Gen. 15:15 "you shall be buried at a good old age."

Ex. 15:26 "For I am the LORD who heals you."

Ex. 12:13 "when I see the blood, I will pass over you; and the plague shall not be on you to destroy you."

Ex. 23:25 "So you shall serve (worship) the LORD your God, and He will bless your bread and your water. And He will take sickness away from the midst of you."

Deut. 23:5 "the LORD your God turned the curse into a blessing for you, because the LORD your God loves you."

Deut. 33:25 "As your days, so shall your strength be."

Ps. 30:2-3 2 "O LORD my God, I cried out to You, And You healed me." **3** " O LORD, You brought my soul up from the grave; You have kept me alive, that I should not go down to the pit."

Ps. 29:11 "I the LORD will give you strength and will bless you with peace."

Ps. 41:2 "I the LORD will preserve you and keep you alive."

Ps. 41:3 "I the LORD will strengthen you on your bed of illness; I will sustain you on your sickbed."

Ps. 91:10 "No evil shall befall you, Nor shall any plague come near your dwelling."

Ps. 91:16 "With long life I will satisfy you."

Ps. 103:3 "I forgive all your iniquities, I heal all your diseases."

Ps. 107:20 "He sent His word and healed you."

Ps. 118:17 "You shall not die, but live, And declare my works."

Ps. 147:3 "I heal the brokenhearted, And bind up their wounds."

Prov. 4:10 "The years of your life will be many."

Prov. 3:8 "Trusting me brings health to your flesh, And strength to your bones."

Prov. 4:22 "My words are life to you, And health/medicine to all your flesh."

Prov. 15:30 "My good report makes your bones healthy."

Prov. 16:24 "My pleasant words are Sweet to your soul and health to your bones."

Neh. 8:10 "My joy is your strength."

Prov. 17:22 "A merry heart does good, like medicine."

Isa. 32:3 "The eyes of those who see will not be dim, And the ears of those who hear will listen."

Isa. 35:5 "Then the eyes of the blind shall be opened, And the ears of the deaf shall be unstopped."

Isa 35:6 "Then the lame shall leap like a deer."

Isa. 32:4 "And the tongue of the stammerers will be ready to speak plainly."

Isa 38:16 "So You will restore me and make me live."

Isa. 40:29 "I give power to the weak, And to those who have no might I increase strength."

Isa 40:31 "But those who wait on the LORD, Shall renew their strength."

Isa. 41:10 "I will strengthen you, Yes, I will help you, I will uphold you with My righteous right hand."

Isa. 53:4 "Surely I bore your griefs (sickness) And I carried your sorrows, (pain)."

Isa. 53:5 "And by my stripes you are healed."

Isa. 57:19 "And I will heal you."

Isa. 58:8 "Then your light shall break forth like the morning, Your healing shall spring forth speedily."

Jer. 30:17 "For I will restore health to you And heal you of your wounds,' says the LORD."

Jer. 33:5-6 "Behold, I will bring it health and healing; I will heal you and reveal to you the abundance of peace and truth."

Jer. 32:27 "Behold, I am the LORD, the God of all flesh. Is there anything too hard for Me?"

Ezek. 34:16 "I will bind up the broken and strengthen what was sick."

Mal. 4:2 "But to you who fear (reverence) My name The Sun of Righteousness shall arise with healing in His wings; And you shall go out and grow fat like stall-fed calves."

Your daily New Testament Prescription:

Matt. 8:3 "I am willing; be cleansed."

Matt. 8:17 "He Himself took your infirmities And bore

your sicknesses."

Matt. 9:12 "Those who are well have no need of a physician, but those who are sick.(I am your physician.)"

Matt. 9:35 "healing every (your) sickness and every (your) disease among the people."

Matt. 10:1 "to heal all kinds of sickness and all kinds of disease."

Matt. 10: 8 "Heal the sick, cleanse the lepers, raise the dead, cast out demons."

Matt. 14:14 "He was moved with compassion for you, and healed you."

Matt. 4:23 "And He went about healing all kinds of sickness and all kinds of disease among the people."

Matt. 12:15 "He healed them all."

Matt. 12:13 "He stretched it out, and it was restored as whole as the other."

Matt. 12:22 "He healed him, so that the blind and mute man both spoke and saw."

Matt. 14:14 "and healed their sick."

Matt. 14:36 And as many as touched it were made perfectly well.

Mark 1:31 "and immediately the fever left her. And she served them."

Mark 1:34 "He healed many who were sick with various diseases."

Mark 1:42 "the leprosy left him, and he was cleansed."

Mark 3:15 "and to have power to heal sicknesses and to cast out demons."

Mark 5:34 "be healed of your affliction."

Mark 6:56 "And as many as touched Him were made well."

Mark 7:37 "And they were astonished beyond measure, saying, "He has done all things well. He makes both the deaf to hear and the mute to speak."

Mark 9:23 "If you can believe, all things are possible to him who believes."

Mark 10:52 " your faith has made you well."

Mark 11:24 "Therefore I say to you, whatever things you ask when you pray, believe that you receive them, and you will have them."

Mark 16:18 "they will lay hands on the sick, and they will recover."

Luke 4:18 "He has sent Me to heal the brokenhearted, And recovery of sight to the blind, To set at liberty those who are oppressed."

Luke 4:40 "He laid His hands on every one of them and healed them."

Luke 6:18 "those who were tormented with unclean spirits. were healed."

Luke 6:19 "power went out from Him and healed them all."

Luke 9:1 " Then He called His twelve disciples together and gave them power and authority over all demons, and to cure diseases."

Luke 9:6 "Healing everywhere."

Luke 9:11 "healed those who had need of healing."

Luke 10:9 "And heal the sick there, and say to them, 'The kingdom of God has come near to you."

Luke 13:12 "Woman, you are loosed from your infirmity."

Luke 14:4 "And He took him and healed him."

Luke18:42-43 "Then Jesus said to him, "Receive your sight; your faith has made you well" And immediately he received his sight, and followed Him, glorifying God."

John 4:50 "Go your way; your son lives. So the man believed the word that Jesus spoke to him, and he went his way."

John 9:6-7 "When He had said these things, He spat on the ground and made clay with the saliva; and He anointed the eyes of the blind man with the clay. And He said to him, "Go, wash in the pool of Siloam" (which is translated, Sent). So he went and washed, and came back seeing."

John 14:13 "And whatever you ask in My name, that I will do, that the Father may be glorified in the Son."

John 15:7 "If you abide in Me, and My words abide in you, you will ask what you desire, and it shall be done for you."

John 16:24 "Ask, and you will receive, that your joy may be full."

Acts 3:6-7 "Then Peter said, "Silver and gold I do not have, but what I do have I give you: In the name of Jesus Christ of Nazareth, rise up and walk." And he took him by the right hand and lifted him up, and immediately his feet and ankle bones received strength."

Acts 5:16 "Sick people and those who were tormented by unclean spirits, and they were all healed."

Acts 8:7 "and many who were paralyzed and lame were healed."

Acts 10:38 "how God anointed Jesus of Nazareth with the Holy Spirit and with power, who went about doing good and healing all who were oppressed by the devil, for God was with Him."

Acts 19:12 "So that even handkerchiefs or aprons were brought from his body to the sick, and the diseases left them and the evil spirits went out of them."

Rom. 10:17 "So then faith comes by hearing, and hearing by the word of God."

1 Cor. 12:28 "And God has appointed these in the church: first apostles, second prophets, third teachers, after that **miracles**, then **gifts of healings**."

Gal. 3:13 "Christ has redeemed us from the curse of the law." (Sickness and disease is a curse)

1 Thess. 5:23 "Now may the God of peace Himself sanctify you completely; and may your whole spirit, soul, and body be preserved blameless at the coming of our Lord Jesus Christ."

Heb. 13:8 "Jesus Christ is the same yesterday, today, and forever."

James 1:17 "Every good gift and every perfect gift is from above, and comes down from the Father of lights."

James 5:14-15 "Is anyone among you sick? Let him call for the elders of the church, and let them pray over him, anointing him with oil in the name of the Lord. And the prayer of faith will save the sick, and the Lord will raise him up. And if he has committed sins, he will be forgiven."

1 Peter 2:24 "Who Himself bore our sins in His own body on the tree, that we, having died to sins, might live for righteousness, **by whose stripes you were healed**."

1 John 5:14-15 "Now this is the confidence that we have in Him, that if we ask anything according to His will, He hears us. 15 And if we know that He hears us, whatever we ask, we know that we have the petitions that we have asked of Him."

3 John 1-2 "Beloved, I pray that you may prosper in all things and **be in health**, just as your soul prospers."

I would like to exhort you to never give up on your healing. It is essential to establish yourself in the Word of God. Faith in the Word of God is what will get you healed.

Remember to attend to His Word and to meditate in it day and night. This will renew your mind and help you to stay in the arena of healing. Our mind has to be renewed to the Word of God for the Word to work in our life.

God has His part to do and we have our part to do. I have set before you life and death, blessing and cursing; therefore choose life. Healing is life; sickness and disease is death. God is telling us to choose life. Jesus said He is life. His Word and faith in His Word will get you healed because there is life and healing in His Holy written Word.

Bibliography

Biblesoft PC Study Bible 2000, <u>Barns' notes.</u>

Biblesoft PC Study Bible2000, <u>New Exhaustive Strongs Concordance.</u>

Biblesoft PC Study Bible 2000, King James Version.

Biblesoft PC Study Bible 2000, <u>Nelsons' Bible Dictionary.</u>

Biblesoft PC Study Bible2000,<u>New American Standard Bible.</u>

Biblesoft PC Study Bible 2000,<u>New American Standard Bible update.</u>

Biblesoft PC Study Bible 2000, <u>New King James Version.</u>

Biblesoft PC Study Bible 2000, <u>Revised Standard Version.</u>

Biblesoft PC Study Bible 2000, <u>Thayer's Greek Lexicon.</u>

Biblesoft PC Study Bible 2000, <u>The Living Bible.</u>

Biblesoft PC Study Bible 2000, <u>Vines Electronic Database.</u>

Bosworth F.F <u>Christ the Healer.</u> Fleming H. Revell Company 1973.

Duffield Guy P. and N.M Van Cleave. <u>Foundations of Pentecostal Theology.</u> Los Angeles, California: Life Bible College 1991.

Hagin, Kenneth E. <u>New thresholds of faith.</u> Tulsa, Oklahoma: Faith Library 1980.

Hagin, Kenneth E. <u>Seven things you should know about Divine healing.</u> Tulsa, Oklahoma: Faith Library 1979.

Hagin, Kenneth Jr. <u>The Untapped Power In Praise.</u> Tulsa, Oklahoma: Faith Library 1991.

Jones, Doug. <u>Understanding the Healing Power of God.</u> Tulsa, Oklahoma: Doug Jones Ministries 1997.

<u>King James Version/Amplified Bible Paralle Edition.</u> Copyright 1995 by the Zondervan Corporation and the Lockman Foundation.

McCrossan Dr. T.J. and Reedited by Roy H. Hicks, D.D., and Kenneth E. Hagin, D.D. <u>Bodily healing and the Atonement.</u> Tulsa Oklahoma: Faith Library 1982.

<u>The New Testament from 26 Translations.</u> Copyright 1967 By Zondervan Publishing House, Grand Rapids, Michigan.

Vine W.E. <u>Vine's Expository Dictionary of New Testament Words.</u> Mclean, Virginia: Mac Donald Publishing Company.

Webster, Merriam. <u>Webster's Ninth New Collegiate Dictionary.</u> Springfield, Massachusetts: Merriam Webster Inc., Publishers 1988.

About the Author

D r. Steven E. Boate is an ordained minister. Graduated from Rhema Bible Training Center, Tulsa, OK in 1992. He received his Ph.D. in Theology from Life Christian University. He is a powerful and anointed teacher and preacher of the Word of God. He has ministered in State and Federal prisons. He has ministered in Mexico as well as in the United States. He and his wife Linda pastor Victory Worship Center in Prescott Valley, Arizona. He also serves as an Professor at the Extension Campus of Life Christian University in Prescott Valley, Arizona.

Dr. Steven Boate and his wife Linda are committed to teaching the body of Christ how to renew their mind to the Word of God and seeing people set free by the Word of God.

Web Site
www.victoryworshipcenteraz.org

E-Mail
vwc@ifriendly.com

CPSIA information can be obtained
at www.ICGtesting.com
Printed in the USA
FSOW01n1641150616
21603FS

9 781594 679407